100
GREAT WAYS TO USE
Rubber Stamps

FRANÇOISE READ

D&C
David and Charles

This book is dedicated to all the people who enjoy crafting and the pleasures it brings. I love to create and design, and it's a blessing I want to share with all of you out there.

A DAVID & CHARLES BOOK
Copyright © David & Charles Limited 2007

David & Charles is an F+W Publications Inc. company
4700 East Galbraith Road
Cincinnati, OH 45236

First published in the UK in 2007

Text and designs copyright © Françoise Read 2007
Photographs copyright © David & Charles 2007

Françoise Read has asserted her right to be identified as author of this work in accordance with the Copyright, Designs and Patents Act, 1988.

A catalogue record for this book is available from the British Library.

ISBN-13: 978-0-7153-2459-2 hardback
ISBN-10: 0-7153-2459-4 hardback

ISBN-13: 978-0-7153-2458-5 paperback
ISBN-10: 0-7153-2458-6 paperback

Printed in People's Republic of China by SNP Leefung for David & Charles
Brunel House   Newton Abbot   Devon

Executive Editor Cheryl Brown
Desk Editor Bethany Dymond
Designer Emma Sandquest
Project Editors Jo Richardson and Betsy Hosegood
Production Controller Kelly Smith
Photographer Karl Adamson

Visit our website at www.davidandcharles.co.uk

David & Charles books are available from all good bookshops; alternatively, you can contact our Orderline on 0870 9908222 or write to us at FREEPOST EX2 110, D&C Direct, Newton Abbot, TQ12 4ZZ (no stamp required UK only); US customers call 800-289-0963 and Canadian customers call 800-840-5220.

Contents

Introduction

Rubber stamping is a simple yet highly versatile craft, as you can see from the 100 unique projects presented in this book. Stamps offer a huge range of ready-to-use images, covering all occasions from birthdays to weddings, popular pastimes such as sports and gardening as well as different styles, both contemporary and traditional. But that's just the beginning! In a series of mini workshops, each of the 25 design sections of the book demonstrates how these stamp motifs and patterns can be applied and enhanced using additional craft techniques and mediums to create not only inventive greetings cards but memorable gifts. Whether you're a beginner, an intermediate or advanced stamper, this is the perfect opportunity to extend your stamping skills and develop your creative repertoire.

Each design chapter opens with a lead project that focuses in detail on the master technique, which is clearly explained in step-by-step instructions and accompanying photographs to ensure success. The following projects offer additional inspirational ideas and explore the technique further to reinforce your new-found expertise. Practical and professional tips are included throughout for extra guidance, quick-reference symbols to help you select projects to suit the occasion (see right for a key), along with templates where required. Product and suppliers details for specific rubber stamps, die-cuts and punches can also be found at the back of the book.

So, all you need to do is choose a technique or project that appeals, pick up your stamp and follow the simple instructions – you will amaze not only family and friends but yourself with your wonderful stamping creations.

What's the occasion?

Use this handy key to identify the cards throughout the book that match the occasion you're celebrating.

	Celebrating baby
	Wish them luck
	Wonderful weddings
	Romance and anniversaries
	Happy birthday
	Celebrations through the year
	Christmas greetings
	Greetings for all
	Exam success
	Children's birthday celebrations
	Bon voyage
	Greetings for men
	Gorgeous gifts

Know Your Stamps

All stamps have a die, which can be made of rubber, polymer or foam and incorporates the image. Stamps are sold individually or in sets, generally on a theme. Most fall into one of the following categories:

Wood mounted

These stamps generally consist of a rubber die, a wooden block and a foam cushion that acts as padding between the die and block, helping to distribute pressure evenly as you press down. There is usually a decal or index of the design on the block.

Clear

Clear stamps are generally sold as unmounted polymer dies in sets, so you need an acrylic block on which to mount the stamp (see pages 36–39). Some clear dies are self-clinging, while others require a non-permanent bonding agent for attaching to the block. Always make sure that the block is larger than the die.

Foam mounted

These stamps usually come in sets and are cheaper to buy, as the components are low-priced. It is worth trimming off the corners to make the stamping process easier.

Unmounted

Some rubber dies are sold separately, either with or without a foam cushion. These dies can be glued to a wooden block together with a foam cushion, or a clear acrylic block, using a non-permanent bonding agent such as Easy Mount™ or a glue stick. These dies are generally quite inexpensive to buy.

Solid stamps

Consisting of a solid rubber mass, most of these stamps have relatively little detail, but are useful for creating backgrounds such as with shadow stamps (see pages 32–35), and work particularly well with mediums such as chalks and brush markers.

Outline stamps

Prints made with these stamps produce the outline of an image, which can be coloured in (see pages 20–23). With some of these stamps, shading in the way of dots or lines comes as part of the image.

Stamping Basics

If you are a newcomer to stamping, begin by mastering the basics. Effective stamping is all about achieving a balance between the amount of ink applied to the rubber and the pressure brought to bear on the mount, which only practice can teach you.

Inking and printing a stamp

1 Check that the rubber is dry and free from dust or hairs. Place the stamp rubber side up on a flat surface. Tap the inkpad gently against the rubber's surface. If the inkpad is new or has recently been re-inked, you will see a quick build-up of ink. Do not press the inkpad against the rubber or too much ink may be released.

2 Hold the stamp up to the light – the wet ink will glisten. Check to see if you have missed any areas and if the ink has been applied evenly. If the stamp has large open areas, clean away any build-up of ink with a cotton bud to avoid any unwanted marks in the final print.

3 Grip the mount on either side with your fingers – use two hands if you are handling a larger stamp. Press rubber side down on your chosen surface using firm, even, downward pressure. Try not to rock the stamp, as this creates double images. Gently lift the stamp away and check the printed image left behind. Leave the print to dry before handling. Alternatively, use a heat gun to quicken the process.

Cleaning stamps

Clean your stamps straight after use. With most stamps you can use water for this. Simply fold up layers of kitchen paper and place them in a shallow tray; dampen the paper and dab your stamp on top. If the stamp ink is not water-soluble, use stamp cleaner. Dab it directly onto the stamp, then wipe off the ink with a clean cloth.

Inking small stamps: If a stamp is considerably smaller than the inkpad you are using, you can tap it directly onto the surface of the pad.

Inking large stamps: A brayer makes it easier to apply an even coating of ink to stamps, especially large ones (see page 108).

Store rubber stamps and polymer dies away from direct sunlight, and don't store anything heavy on top of rubber stamps to avoid squashing the cushion.

Trouble shooting

• If the print is uneven and patchy with areas missing, you are applying insufficient and uneven pressure.

• If the print is over-heavy and blurred, you are applying too much pressure or too much ink and rocking the stamp.

Know Your Inkpads

It is important to select the right type of ink for the surface you are stamping. Most come with guidance on use, but it is always wise to do a test print. Available in a variety of sizes and shapes, most inkpads have a raised sponge or felt pad that makes it easy to ink up any size of stamp. Some come in single colours, while others are multicoloured.

Dye-based inks

These are water-based, mainly non-permanent and usually have a felt pad. They are available in a variety of single-colour or multicoloured pads. Dye-based inks are translucent and fast drying, and can be stamped on most types of card, but work best on glossy paper (see pages 108–111).

Fast-drying pigment inks

These are thick, creamy and opaque, and usually come with a foam pad. Brilliance™ and Mica Magic™ inkpads are good examples, which can be used on a variety of unusual surfaces such as vellum (see pages 52–55) and shrink plastic (see pages 104–107). As these inks dry quickly, they are not suitable for heat embossing.

Embossing inks

Clear or slightly tinted, most embossing inks come with a foam pad. They are designed to dry slowly so that you can use them with opaque, glitter or metallic embossing powders.

Slow-drying pigment inks

These have a similar consistency to fast-drying pigment inks, but their slow-drying quality makes them ideal for heat embossing (see pages 28–31).

Permanent/ solvent-based inks

Permanent inks are available in both water- and solvent-based forms and can be used on most types of card, as well as wood, acetate, glass (see pages 100–103), shrink plastic, metal foil (see pages 76–78), leather and acrylic.

Resist inks

These are formulated to resist or repel water-based dye inks on glossy paper (see pages 108–111). The VersaMark™ inkpad can also be used to create a watermark or a tone-on-tone effect. It can also act as an adhesive for chalks and Perfect Pearls™ (see pages 56–59), and is suitable for heat embossing.

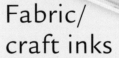

Fabric/ craft inks

Some fabric inks are designed primarily for use with fabric, while other types, such as Crafter's™ and VersaCraft™, are multipurpose and can also be used on wood, leather, shrink plastic and unglazed ceramics. Heat setting with an iron is required on fabric, especially if stamping clothing (see pages 96–99).

Don't replace an old inkpad – buy re-fill inks, which can also be used like ink paint.

Tools & Materials

Beyond the basic tools you need, you might also want to acquire some more specialist tools as you progress in your stamping. You will also need a range of materials for constructing your cards and gift items, and to add colour and decoration.

Basic tools

The tools itemized below are used throughout the book. If you are a regular crafter, you are likely to have many of these items already.

Scissors (1) After a craft knife, the next most important tool you need is a sharp pair of scissors. We all have our favourite pair, so find some that suit you and keep them safe.

Pencil (2) Use for marking measurements on paper and card. Keep the point sharp for accuracy, or use a propelling pencil. Avoid very soft-leaded pencils, as they are harder to erase.

Eraser (3) Make sure that your eraser doesn't smudge and is clean before use.

Pencil sharpener (4) Use a good-quality sharpener that doesn't chew up the wood – important when sharpening expensive colouring or watercolour pencils. One with a case is useful for keeping your work space clean.

Bone folder (5) This tool will help you achieve crisp, neat folds when scoring and folding card (see page 14).

Ruler (6) A transparent plastic ruler is ideal for measuring and marking. A metal ruler should be used when trimming card with a craft knife. Some plastic rulers have a metal strip down one edge.

Craft knife (7) Ideal for trimming card and cutting out intricate designs. Purchase one with disposable blades – a blunt blade can hinder the cutting process. Always use with a self-healing cutting mat.

Self-healing cutting mat (8) In addition to cutting, these mats are very useful as a base for stamping, although never use with a heat gun. Protect when stamping to keep it clean.

Paper trimmer (9) There are many different types available, so look for one that suits your crafting purposes. It is an invaluable investment, especially when you progress to regular card making.

Paintbrushes (10) Keep a selection of different-sized and -shaped paintbrushes for applying colour to your stamping in a variety of ways. Quality is important, but fairly decent nylon brushes are available at a reasonable price. Store in a pouch or tube, and never leave standing in water.

Sponge daubers (11) These are designed to fit on your index finger and are used to apply inks to backgrounds and stamped images. Although ordinary sponges can be used instead, the sponged effect is more even and your hands stay clean.

Holepunches (12) These come in a variety of sizes, but 1.5mm (1/16in), 4mm (1/8in) and 6mm (1/4in) are the most useful. Use to make holes for brads, eyelets, wire and ribbon. For hard-to-reach places, you could invest in an 'anywhere' holepunch.

Heat gun (13) Use to melt embossing powders (see pages 28–31), heat shrink plastic (see pages 104–107), set inks (see page 92) and to dry work in progress. Proceed with care and protect your work surface from the intense heat.

Embossing tool (14) This tool can be used to score card (see page 14), 'frost' vellum (see pages 52–55) and to emboss metal foil (see pages 76–78). It comes in fine, medium and large ball sizes. When using on vellum, work over a foam mat.

Paper piercer (15) Useful for making holes in card for sewing or for brads – by controlling the piercing you can make the holes smaller or larger.

Corner rounder punch (16) An invaluable tool for rounding the corners of card, which is difficult to do accurately with scissors.

Tweezers (17) Ideal for lifting and holding delicate items such as gems and stickers or for pulling ribbon and threads through punched holes.

Anti-static puff (18) Used to wipe the card before stamping and embossing to reduce the static, which holds stray specks of powder on the surface. It also helps to counteract any moisture absorbed by the card.

Specialist tools

You will find that you need more specialist tools when you begin to develop your stamping skills beyond the basics. Die-cutting systems are relatively expensive, but are very useful for cutting letters, apertures and basic as well as more elaborate shapes quickly and accurately. Punches offer a cheaper alternative. For setting eyelets, a hard mat, setting tool and hammer are essential. Wire cutters and round-nosed pliers are required for working with wire when making jewellery pieces, for example.

Adhesives

Different types of glue are needed for mounting card and paper and for adhering embellishments. Use a glue stick or double-sided adhesive tape for mounting and Hi-Tack Glue™ or PVA (white) glue for embellishments – apply small dots with a cocktail stick. Adhesive foam pads or silicone glue are useful for 3-D découpage (see pages 68–71) or where you want to raise an element on a card. You can also purchase special glue dispensers such as a Xyron™ machine. Always check that the adhesive will work on a trial piece of the card or other surface.

Embossing powders

These are heated and melted to achieve a raised outline or surface on stamped images (see pages 28–31), and bring a real wow factor to stamping. They are available in every colour imaginable, and in glitter and metallic forms, but gold, silver and clear are the most useful for beginners.

Colouring mediums

The more colouring mediums you combine with your stamping, the greater the range of effects you will achieve. Brush markers can be used direct from the pen or as a watercolour medium to colour in stamped images, or applied to a stamp's rubber, so they are ideal for beginners. Subtle shading can be achieved with colouring and watercolour pencils, while chalks and Perfect Pearls™ produce soft tonal and pearlescent effects.

Embellishments

These provide the decorative detail and finishing touches to your stamped designs, as well as additional colour and textural interest. The huge range available makes it easy to find just the right item to complement your scheme. Some embellishments such as brads and ribbon are functional as well as decorative.

Card & Papers

If you are starting out in rubber stamping, card and paper are the easiest and most popular surfaces to stamp on. I recommend stamping on thin card, then mounting and layering with thin card and papers onto a folded card, so that if you make a mistake, you won't have wasted a folded card.

Making the right choice

It is important to know how to choose what card and papers to use. But with such an abundance of choice available, this selection process can be somewhat daunting, especially as a beginner. The following is a guide to the various issues you need to consider to help you make the right choice.

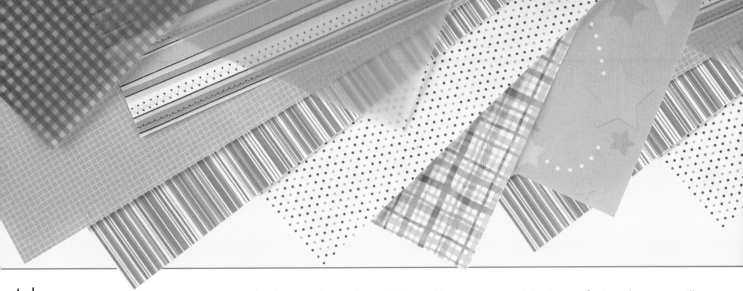

Ink

Is your inkpad suitable for the paper and card you wish to use – will it dry on the surface? For example, if you use slow-drying pigment inks (see page 7) on glossy paper (see pages 108–110) or vellum (see pages 52–55), you will need to emboss the ink, as it cannot be absorbed and therefore will not dry on these surfaces.

Absorbency

Most card and papers absorb moisture but at different rates, unless they are coated. How long will the ink take to dry – will it dry too fast to heat emboss (see pages 28–31)? For example, if you want to stamp and emboss on watercolour paper, you need to take into account that it is highly absorbent, so the ink may dry out too quickly for the powder to adhere properly.

Density

The density does not refer to the weight of the card or paper but to its flexibility and the compactness of the fibres that gives it its strength. You can gauge the degree of density by checking whether or not it folds easily, if it is too hard to score or if you can tear it.

Finish

Some card and papers are not coated but left plain and matt, while others may have a glossy, metallic or pearlescent finish. How the surface of the card is finished will also help determine the type of inkpad you use if you intend to work directly on the surface.

Texture

Card and papers can be smooth or textured. It is easier to stamp on a smooth, flat surface, but a small degree of texture can be tolerated. If the card or paper is heavily textured, such as with glittered card, it is best to use it purely for layering and mounting. Popular textures include linen-effect, hammered and corrugated. Mounting on textured card always adds visual interest to a design.

Weight

Generally, the thicker the card or paper, the greater it weighs. When mounting your designs, consider whether the card is thick enough to make a folded card or should be used purely for layering. Is it thin enough to use for building up several layers when mounting? Bear in mind in this case that the folded card will need to be strong enough to support these applied layers without toppling over.

Acid-free and archival

If you want to create designs that can be preserved for the future, you need to select card and papers that are acid-free and archival. Most manufacturers, especially those of printed papers, will specify which of their products are acid-free and archival, so that you can purchase with confidence. However, if in doubt, ask the supplier.

Cost and quality

If you intend to sell your stamped creations to raise money for yourself or charity, you need to take into account the cost of each card blank used and achieve a balance between quality and cost. If the card looks cheap, it might adversely affect sales, or if it is too expensive, you will lose any profit. Buying in bulk is often cheaper. If buying by mail order or online, try to obtain swatches first to judge the look and feel of the card.

Storage

Consider where you are going to store your card and papers. You need to be able to store them away from direct sunlight and in a dry environment. You might only have the space to store card that is A4 (US letter) in size, so if you buy larger pieces, you will need a suitable cutter to trim them down.

Some card suppliers manufacture clear plastic wallets to fit their blank cards, which are ideal for storing your work in progress.

Other Surfaces

Once you feel confident stamping on card and paper, begin experimenting with other mediums, as featured in the later sections of this book.

Fabric

Smooth weaves, such as silk and cotton, will give you the best stamping results (see pages 96–99). If stamping on an item of clothing, always wash the fabric to remove the sizing and to avoid shrinking the design. If you intend colouring in a stamped outline on fabric, heat set the stamping with an iron so that the ink does not bleed. Fabric accessories such as canvas shoes and bags can also be stamped.

Polymer clay

Polymer clay, such as Sculpey™ and Fimo™, can be stamped and, unlike wet clay, are easy to work with and can be baked in an ordinary oven. You can also use moulds to create polymer clay embellishments for your stamped designs (see Butterfly Dreams, page 115). Polymer clays are also ideal for creating items of jewellery and Christmas ornaments (see Silver Tree Ornament, pages 112–114). If you enjoy working with clay, instead of rolling it out with a rolling pin, you could invest in a pasta machine.

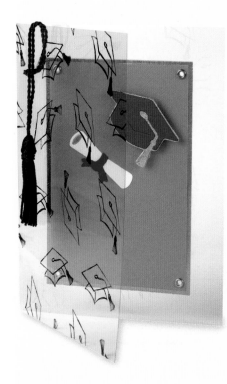

Acetate and glass

Acetate is a thin plastic that comes in ready-to-use sheets. As it is transparent, it is useful for layering stamped images on top of each other or over interesting background papers (see pages 100–102). Eyelets and brads work best to attach it to card. Because of the popularity of glass painting, there are many glass objects available that are suitable for stamping. As the smooth surface is quite difficult to stamp on, start with a flat shape, such as a heart, oval or diamond (see Floral Sun Catcher, page 103). Do not stamp on eating or drinking surfaces.

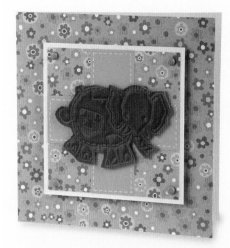

Fun foam

This type of foam is highly compact and available in a variety of colours. It comes in thin sheets that are easy to cut up or as pre-cut shapes, such as flowers and butterflies. You can heat the surface carefully with a heat gun and stamp into the foam to create a relief print (see Nellie the Elephant, page 79). The relief print can also be used as a stamp.

Metal

Tin metals or thin sheets of metal foil are suitable to stamp on. Metal foil comes in a variety of colours and its surface can be easily drawn into with an embossing tool to create an embossed image (see Oh, Christmas Tree, pages 76–77). Permanent ink and pens must be used when working on metal.

Mountboard, chipboard and Mini Matts™

These materials are manufactured from layers of card, which make them very strong and able to withstand the intense heat applied in enamelling (see pages 84–87). Mountboard is normally used for picture frame mounts, so offcuts are available from framing shops. Chipboard (thick cardboard) and Mini Matts™ come pre-cut in a variety of shapes, such as hearts, letters and circles (see Copper-plated Notebook, pages 84–85, and Butterfly Brooch, page 86). If you enjoy enamelling and working with these products, consider investing in a Ranger Melting Pot™ for melting the enamelling powder.

Wood

Wood can be unfinished (untreated and bare) or finished (varnished and sealed or painted), but the former is harder to stamp on. Ideally, the surface needs to be sanded down to a smooth finish and a light coat of varnish applied to stop the ink from bleeding (see Goal!, page 95). A wide range of unfinished wooden items are available from craft stores, such as trays, simple shapes and boxes (see Jade Trinket Box, page 78).

Shrink plastic

Shrink plastic is great fun to experiment with. Available in translucent, opaque white, clear and black, it can be stamped, coloured, cut out and then heated with a heat gun or baked to make jewellery, badges, buttons and miniature panels (see pages 104–107). It offers the opportunity to use large stamps, since the images are greatly reduced after heating. If the plastic is not pre-sanded, you will need to sand it yourself before using. As several manufacturers produce shrink plastic, it is important to follow the specific product's instructions.

Style stones

These are inkable, cultured stones that come in two finishes, coated and natural. The coated stones are ivory in colour and have flat surfaces that are ideal for sponging and stamping (see Hats Galore, page 94). The natural stones are white and have engraved surfaces. These are ideal for simple stamped designs and colouring. Both can be used on cards or to create jewellery pieces (see Dragonfly Brooch, page 92).

Making a Folded Card

Although there is a huge range of pre-scored and folded cards on the market in a variety of sizes and colours, it is very useful to be able to score and fold your own cards in a professional way. You may, for instance, create a design without a folded card size in mind and therefore need to tailor-make a folded card so that the presentation is perfect. It can also be cheaper to buy sheets of card in bulk, in which case you need to cut them down and make up the cards yourself. On other occasions, you may simply not be able to find a folded card in the colour or finish you want.

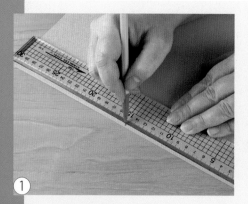

①

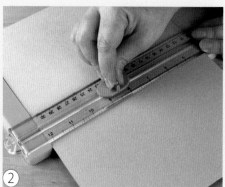

②

③

Check if the card has a definite right side, such as a texture or print, then turn over and score on the wrong side.

1 Use a pencil and ruler to measure and mark the card for cutting. Until you become accustomed to using a paper trimmer, it is best to use this method, as it is easy to make cutting mistakes and waste card. Later, you can calculate the size using the measurements on the trimmer.

2 Place the card in a paper trimmer, aligning the pencil marks to where the blade will cut. Alternatively, if you want to use a craft knife, place the card on a cutting mat and use a metal ruler to line up the marks and cut the card. Both the craft knife and trimmer blades need to be sharp.

3 Match up the opposite corners of the trimmed card. Hold these carefully in place as you press down to create the central fold. On thick card, mark the fold and then score with a medium ball embossing tool. Run the flat edge of a bone folder over the fold to give a neat finish.

Making the Most of One Stamp

Good presentation is the cornerstone of making your stamping look professional, and much satisfaction can be gained from producing the best results. Presentation includes the layout, colour scheme and materials used, which all work together to create the final design. The samples below show you how you can take a single stamp and, by altering the presentation, produce several very different designs. Never think that you can only make one card with one stamp!

Adhesive foam pads have been used to raise the main stamped image. The heart offers an alternative approach to the usual layering of rectangular frames, and brings an instant romantic flavour to the design.

The circular aperture helps to frame the main stamped image, and punched flowers add a decorative touch. The red bows echo the red of the card frame, and the overall effect is more casual.

By stamping the image on a long, narrow, landscape-shaped card, its appearance changes again and allows space either side for the punched hearts.

A tag has been made from the stamped image, and the colour scheme restricted to subtle greys and teals.

A panel has been added below the main stamped image, covered with printed paper, which could be used for a stamped message. The cats look more formal left white except for the bows.

Notice how the colours of the bows that the cats are wearing remain the focal point of each design.

The cats have been coloured to complement the colours of the printed paper used as a background. The card used for layering also coordinates with the striking colour scheme.

Pens

If you have no inkpad, you can still produce a print from a stamp using pens. Simply apply colour to the rubber using the tip of a marker or felt-tip pen – brush markers with a broad nib work best. You can apply as little or as much colour detail as you require, and choose to use only part of an image. This technique is easy to master and produces instant results.

You will need ■ hearts on stems rubber stamp ■ brush markers – vermilion, crimson, green, spring green ■ white linen-effect card ■ red mirror card ■ lime green card 17 x 7cm (6¾ x 2¾in) ■ white linen-effect folded card 18 x 8cm (7 x 3¼in) ■ tag punch ■ holographic glitter glue ■ gold eyelet ■ white sheer ribbon

①

②

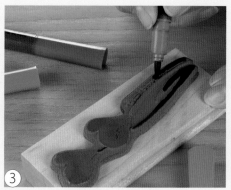
③

1 Using the tip of the vermilion brush maker, carefully apply areas of colour to the top heart of the stamp's rubber. Fill the gaps that are left with the crimson brush marker.

2 Lift the stamp towards your mouth and breathe over the rubber – this will revive the colours if they have dried out during application. Check that the rubber looks shiny, then make a print of the heart on one piece of the white card.

3 Clean the rubber to remove any residue of ink using water or stamp cleaner. Repeat the application process, but this time colour in the stems with the brush markers in two shades of green as well as both the hearts.

1 Blooming Hearts

Use brush markers to apply different shades of a colour to a rubber stamp and print onto textured paper.

In this case, hearts and stems have been stamped in vibrant red and green tones – always remember to apply the lightest colour to the rubber first. A tag stamped with one heart from the design adds a simple yet effective finishing touch, and could be used to add a secret message or a declaration of love!

You can leave the stamped images without diluting and blending the colours if you prefer the textured effect.

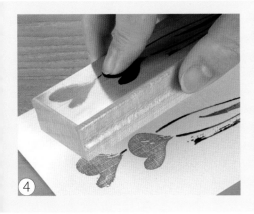

4 Lift the stamp towards your mouth and breathe over the rubber. Again check that the rubber looks shiny, then make a print centrally on a separate piece of the white card. The print will show the linen-like texture of the card.

5 Dip a fine paintbrush into clean water and paint over the two hearts to blend the reds and fill in the gaps left by the texture of the card. As you paint, allow some of the colour to flow beyond the edges of the hearts. Repeat with the single heart and stems of the main image. Leave to dry.

6 Punch out the single heart with the tag punch, held upside down to centre it. Squeeze the glitter glue bottle gently and hold a little way above the image to allow the glue to flow out and highlight the hearts. Leave to dry. Trim the main image card to 14 x 6cm (5½ x 2³⁄₈in).

To Finish

⑦ *Mount the main stamped panel on a slightly larger piece of red mirror card. Secure the ribbon to the back of the red card.*

⑧ *Mount the lime green card on the front of the folded card, then mount the stamped panel towards the top of the folded card.*

⑨ *Punch a hole in the top of the tag with a 4mm (⅛in) holepunch and set the eyelet in the hole (see page 101). Thread the tag onto the ribbon and tie around the main stamped panel in a bow.*

---

2 Make a Wish

Try using your pens on an outline stamp to achieve colour detail in the line.

The pens applied to the rubber are also used here to colour in the cake image, but first diluted with water for a softer look.

You will need ■ slice of cake with candle rubber stamp ■ brush markers – yellow, orange, tan, pink, peony ■ white linen-effect and white card ■ fuchsia folded card 12cm (4¾in) square ■ spotted printed vellum 10cm (4in) square ■ yellow pearlescent paper ■ brads – 2 pink, 2 yellow ■ die-cutting tool and streamer and confetti die ■ holographic glitter glue

> *Always clean the stamp before re-applying colours to make further prints, as it is hard to see where you have used specific pens.*

1 Using the tips of the brush markers, apply the colours to the stamp's rubber. Start with the lightest and work through to the darkest. Breathe over the rubber. Check that it looks shiny, then print onto white linen-effect card.

2 Run each brush marker over a plastic lid. Dip a fine paintbrush into clean water, pick up some of the ink and fill in some of the open spaces within the cake and candle. Don't use too much water or the outline will dissolve. Cut out, leaving a narrow border.

3 Mount a 9cm (3½in) square of white card onto the front of the folded card. Put a dab of glue stick in the centre. Place the vellum centrally over the square – any glue that shows through will be hidden by the cake.

4 Punch a hole in each corner of the card panel with a 1.5mm (1/16in) holepunch and insert a brad. Mount the cake with adhesive foam pads. Die-cut streamers and confetti from the pearlescent paper (see pages 40–43). Glue around the cake. Highlight the flame and icing with the glitter glue.

3 Blue Vases

Use a fine water spray to mix and blend the colours on the rubber before printing.

Although this technique requires practice, the outcome is well worth it, and one spray is all you need to make several prints in one go.

Protect your work area, as some of the water will splatter off the stamp when spraying.

You will need ■ flowers in vases rubber stamp ■ brush markers – yellow, orange, spring green, green, blue, dark blue, purple ■ white linen-effect card 14.5cm (5¾in) square ■ yellow, blue, orange and green card ■ lime green folded card 14.5cm (5¾in) square ■ die-cutting tool and flower and stem die ■ water spray with fine nozzle

1 Using the tips of the brush markers, apply the colours to the stamp's rubber. Start with the lightest and work through to the darkest. Point the nozzle of the water spray towards the rubber from a reasonable distance away and spray a very delicate mist onto the surface – too much water will make the colours too runny for a clear print.

2 Print the stamp onto the white card. Continue making prints until the colours run dry – each print will become lighter. Trim your favourite print down to a panel 10cm (4in) square and mount onto a slightly larger piece of yellow card.

3 Tear down one edge of a blue card strip, then mount down the left-hand side of the folded card. Tear an orange card strip and mount next to the blue strip, leaving a gap in between. Mount the stamped panel on the card. Die-cut flowers and stems from green card (see pages 40–43). Form decorative crosses with the stems and a border with a row of the flowers.

4 Funky Fish

Using pens and a water spray, make multiple prints to build up a creative design.

One print of a block of cubes was used here for the backdrop, and the remaining prints for stamping fish onto, to create a retro sixties-style card.

Enliven a design with a contrasting colour, such as the turquoise card used here to frame the stamped panel.

You will need ■ rubber stamps – block of cubes; fish ■ brush markers – yellow, orange, terracotta, dark brown ■ graphite black Brilliance™ inkpad ■ white linen-effect card ■ orange card ■ turquoise card 9cm (3½in) square ■ brown folded card 16 x 11cm (6¼ x 4½in) ■ orange cotton cord ■ die-cutting tool and circles dies ■ water spray with fine nozzle

1 Using the tips of the brush markers, apply the colours to the cubes stamp. Start with the lightest and work through to the darkest. Lightly mist the rubber surface with the water spray. Make several prints onto the white card. Using the black inkpad, stamp three fish onto the boldest print and cut out.

2 Run each brush marker over a plastic lid. Select another print. Use a wet fine paintbrush and the pen ink to fill in some of the open spaces of the image. Trim and mount on orange card. Tear the edges of the orange card to leave a narrow border. Mount onto the turquoise card.

3 Wrap the cord three times around the folded card front. Spread out and tie together on the front and inside. Mount the panel on the card with adhesive foam pads. Mount the fish, raising the two on the panel. Add circles die-cut from orange card (see pages 40–43).

Adding Colour

Once an outline has been stamped, you can enjoy adding a personal creative touch with colour. Which medium you choose depends on the required outcome and ease of application. Colour can be applied wet in the form of paints or dry using pencils, and by employing a variety of techniques, such as layering wet paint and blending pencil colours, you will maximize the full potential of your stamps.

You will need ■ baby hedgehog in hammock rubber stamp ■ graphite black Brilliance™ inkpad ■ Vivid™ Mini inkpads – spring green, green, raspberry, purple, yellow, orange, brown ■ white card ■ lilac card ■ white folded card 14.5cm (5¾in) square ■ lilac gingham paper ■ punches – flower, 1cm (³⁄₈in) circle, tag ■ lilac and white spotted ribbon ■ holographic glitter glue ■ large piece of kitchen foil

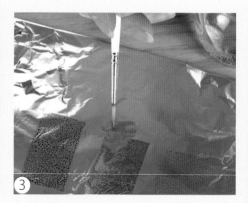

1 Using the black inkpad, ink the stamp up carefully. Check that there is ink all over the rubber, then stamp onto white card. Repeat to make a second print. Allow both prints to dry thoroughly before starting to paint.

2 Lay the piece of foil out flat. Gently press the surface of each mini inkpad in turn against the foil. Make each print at least 1cm (³⁄₈in) apart to avoid the colours running into each other.

3 Dip a fine paintbrush into clean water and pick up the first colour from the foil palette – the water on the end of the brush will dilute the ink, and if the ink has dried on the foil, it will reactivate it. Test the intensity of the colour on scrap card first.

Use your inkpads to create a unique colour palette for watercolour painting.

By layering the washes of colour, you will add depth and bring the design to life – and the good news is that most inkpads can be used in this way. To create a special card to welcome a new baby girl, I added further depth by cutting out and raising sections of the stamped design to make them three-dimensional. This card can be easily adapted for a baby boy.

You can use a large plastic lid instead of the foil as a painting palette, or use an old CD if using fewer or smaller inkpads.

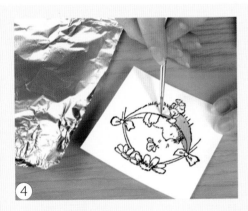

(4)

(5)

(6)

4 Starting with one section at a time, such as the hammock, apply a light wash all over. Work on both images at the same time so that you can make them as identical as possible.

5 To add shading to the colour-washed section, apply more colour to some areas to make them darker by picking up less water and more ink from the palette. Use extra water to blend in the edges of the darker areas.

6 Continue to use washes of colour to fill in all the sections of the image. To make a flesh colour for the baby hedgehog's face, tummy and feet, mix a small, equal amount of orange and pink ink together.

To Finish

(8)
Trim one hedgehog image to a panel 8.5cm (3½in) square. Cut out around the daisies. Now cut around the front of the hammock, hedgehog, teddy bear and bows of the other image to create another cutout. Using adhesive foam pads, layer the cutouts over the corresponding areas of the base panel.

(7)
Cover the back and left-hand side of the folded card with gingham paper. Glue a strip of lilac card down the right-hand edge.

(9)
Mount the panel on a slightly larger piece of lilac card, then onto the folded card with adhesive foam pads.

(10)
Punch a tag from lilac card, cover half with the gingham paper and add a white punched daisy with a punched circle for the centre. Punch a hole with a 4mm (⅛in) holepunch. Thread onto the ribbon and tie around the card.

(11)
Highlight the hedgehog, hammock and daises with the glitter glue.

(12)
Add three punched daisies for a mini border.

Use colouring pencils to bring a real sense of depth to a stamped landscape.

To create a colourful bon voyage card, carefully choose a light and dark tone, to add dimension to all the elements of the scene and achieve the feeling of distance.

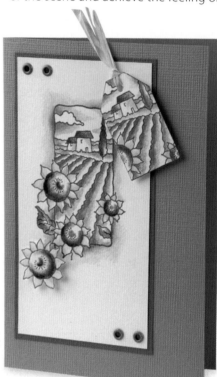

You will need

■ landscape with sunflowers rubber stam■
■ coffee bean Brillianc■ inkpad ■ colouring pencils ■ cream card
■ dark brown card
■ light brown folded card 15 x 10cm (6 x 4in)
■ tag punch ■ raffia
■ 4 lilac eyelets

Use soft-leaded colouring pencils for effective blending and a good pencil sharpener to maintain a sharp point.

1 Using the brown inkpad, stamp the landscape design three times onto cream card. Using colouring pencils, colour in two complete images and just the large sunflower head of the third.

2 Trim down one image to a panel 12.5 x 6.5cm (5 x 2½in). Punch a tag from the second image and cut out the sunflower head from the third. Punch a hole in the top of the tag with a 4mm (⅛in) holepunch. Press the edges of the tag onto the brown inkpad to colour them. Thread the tag hole with a length of raffia and tie in a knot.

3 Mount the main panel on a slightly larger piece of dark brown card, then onto the folded card to the left of centre as shown in the photo. Set two eyelets in the top left-hand and bottom right-hand corners of the cream panel (see page 101). Mount the tag and sunflower head with adhesive foam pads.

7 Shimmering Fall

Create a striking stained-glass effect with Perfect Pearls™ on dark card.

By embossing the stamped image, you create a raised outline that forms a barrier, making it easier to paint the separate sections of this seasonal design in different colours.

If you accidentally paint onto the embossed lines, simply remove the paint with a piece of damp kitchen paper.

You will need ■ 3 stained glass-style oak leaves and acorn set of rubber stamps ■ VersaMark™ inkpad ■ clear embossing powder ■ Perfect Pearls™ – sunflower sparkle, kiwi, plum, berry twist ■ black card 9cm (3½in) square ■ gold mirror card ■ olive green pearlescent card ■ blue pearlescent folded card 13cm (5in) square ■ filmstrip border punch ■ 4 metallic green square brads

1 Using the VersaMark™ inkpad, stamp the three stamps onto the black card, then heat emboss with clear embossing powder (see pages 28–31).

2 To paint this design, four colours of Perfect Pearls™ were used straight from the pot. Select a colour and, using a fine paintbrush, place a small amount of powder onto a palette. Use the same paintbrush to pick up a couple of drops of clean water to mix with the powder to create a liquid paint. Add the water gradually so that you avoid waste and are able to control the mixing process. Test the density of the colour before applying to the stamped images.

3 Use the filmstrip border punch to punch tiny gold rectangles. Stick on the panel. Mount onto a slightly larger piece of olive green pearlescent card. Using a 1.5mm (¹⁄₁₆in) holepunch, punch holes in the black panel corners and insert brads. Mount on a slightly larger piece of the gold card with adhesive foam pads, then onto the folded card.

8 Cheers

Use colour in a more abstract, experimental way by mixing coordinating tones and applying and blending at random over a stamped image.

This technique is ideal when working with detailed images that would otherwise require lots of filling in.

Watercolour paper works best with this technique, as the structure of other papers restricts the flow and quantity of surface water that can be used.

You will need ■ wine bottles and glasses rubber stamp ■ VersaMark™ inkpad ■ white embossing powder ■ pre-mixed concentrated watercolour paints – yellow, spring and forest green, navy blue ■ watercolour paper ■ dark blue card ■ corrugated lime green card 14.5 x 10cm (5¾ x 4in) ■ dark blue folded card 15 x 10.5cm (6 x 4¼in) ■ die-cutting tool and wine bottle, glass and cork dies ■ 2 white eyelets

1 Using the inkpad, stamp the image onto watercolour paper, then heat emboss with white embossing powder (see pages 28–31).

2 Apply a water wash all over. Apply yellow paint with a medium paintbrush over random areas. Repeat with the light and dark greens through to blue, applying less each time. Highlight details in dark green and blue.

3 Cut out the image and mount onto a slightly larger piece of dark blue card, then onto the green corrugated card and in turn onto the folded card. Set an eyelet in each top corner of the panel (see page 101). Die-cut a wine bottle, two glasses and a cork from dark blue card (see pages 40–43), glue one glass and the cork to the card, then mount the bottle and second glass with adhesive foam pads.

Colour Schemes

Using colour in a considered way can greatly enhance your work, and allow you to make the most of your stamps. Understanding how different colours react with one another is key to guiding you in what to choose and what to avoid in any scheme. It is invariably easier to achieve a harmonious colour composition by limiting the number of colours you use in a particular design.

You will need ■ chick and hats rubber stamp ■ royal blue VersaColor™ inkpad ■ pearl blue embossing powder ■ blue Sakura Starlight™ pen ■ white linen-effect card ■ blue and dark blue card ■ pale blue card 13 x 20cm (5 x 8in), plus scraps ■ scraps of printed papers ■ plain blue and blue plaid ribbon ■ die-cutting tool and hat dies

(1)

(2)

(3)

1 Using the inkpad, ink the chick stamp up carefully. Check that there is ink all over the rubber, then stamp onto the white linen-effect card.

2 Sprinkle the embossing powder all over the wet stamped image. Tip away the excess powder, returning it to the jar. Check that the image is completely covered and carefully remove any stray powder with a paintbrush. Using a heat gun, heat the surface of the powder (see page 29).

3 Run the glaze pen over scrap paper – the flow will be quicker than on plastic, and speed is of the essence, as you must use the ink before it dries out. Dip a fine paintbrush into clean water and pick up some of the ink. Test the intensity of the diluted colour on scrap paper.

Try restricting a design to using only the shades of a single colour to create a simple, subtle scheme.

The advantage of this type of approach to colour is that it can be used with any image. Just decide on a particular colour and get started! Look out for packs of monochromatic card, which will make it easier for you to coordinate your layout. Here, I have chosen blue as the colour theme for this fun, springtime design, which is perfect for Easter.

When using simple colour schemes, incorporate a variety of different materials and textures, as well as colouring mediums, to add interest.

4 Starting with one section at a time, such as the chick, flower or one of the hats, apply a light wash to one side to create shading. This will make them look more three-dimensional. When returning to a section to add more shading, pick up less water and more ink.

5 Apply very light colour washes in patches to the background, leaving a white halo around the image. Apply a little more colour below the chick for ground. Trim the card to 10 x 7.5cm (4 x 3in). Stick ribbon across the bottom with Hi-Tack Glue™. Mount on a slightly larger piece of blue card.

6 Score and fold two flaps 5cm (2in) wide in the pale blue card. Mount the panel inside. Die-cut and assemble two hats from dark and pale blue card and printed papers. Mount one on the inside, the other on one flap with an adhesive foam pad. Glue ribbon to the card back, to tie in front.

10 You're a Star

Experiment with using two contrasting colours to create a vibrant scheme.

Purple and yellow are opposite each other on the colour wheel, so create maximum impact when combined. I have used shades of both colours for this striking congratulatory card to extend the palette.

You will need ■ girl on a star swing rubber stamp ■ graphite black Brilliance™ inkpad ■ brush markers – purple, yellow, orange ■ smooth white card ■ purple and yellow card ■ pale lilac folded card 14.5 x 10.5cm (5¾ x 4¼in) ■ mini star punch ■ holographic glitter glue

1 Using the inkpad, stamp the image onto smooth white card. Run each brush marker over a plastic lid. Dip a fine paintbrush into clean water, pick up some of the ink and fill in the image and part of the background. Trim the card to 10.5 x 7cm (4¼ x 2¾in).

2 Mount the panel on a piece of purple card 11.5 x 8cm (4½ x 3¼in). Stick some strips of yellow card in varying widths vertically and horizontally across the front of the folded card for decoration.

3 Mount the stamped panel on the folded card. Add some stars punched from yellow and purple card to the background around the girl and star and in a row in the bottom right-hand corner of the card. Highlight the star and the girl's hair, dress and shoes with the glitter glue.

A black outline is always best to use in a scheme where you want to create contrast.

11 The Happy Couple

For a contemporary approach, use whites, greys and blacks in your colour scheme.

I chose a bold, graphic stamp design here, which is enhanced by the striking colour scheme. The black and clear gems and silver threads add a touch of glamour.

You will need ■ bride and groom rubber stamp ■ graphite black Brilliance™ inkpad ■ smooth white card ■ black card ■ white linen-effect folded card 16 x 11cm (6¼ x 4¼in) ■ black, grey and white striped printed paper ■ black and clear gems ■ silver thread

1 Using the inkpad, ink up the stamp carefully – check that there is ink all over the rubber, as this image has large solid areas. Stamp onto smooth white card.

2 Using a wet paintbrush, pick up a tiny amount of ink from the side of the inkpad. Test the intensity of the diluted colour before shading in the roses on the bouquet. Trim the card to 13.5 x 8cm (5¼ x 3¼in) and mount on a slightly larger piece of black card.

3 Cover the outside of the folded card with the striped paper. Mount the panel on the card. Add a black gem to each corner of the panel and clear gems to the groom's shirt front and lady's ear. Tie a length of silver thread in a bow and glue below the floral bouquet.

Check carefully for any specks of dust or hairs that may be on a solid stamp before inking, as these instantly show up on a print.

Use a printed background paper as a guide to colouring a central stamped design.

This scheme uses mainly primary colours, and when used in combination at their most intense, they create a bold, cheerful effect – perfect for an encouraging good-luck message. To create a truly unique gift item, I have devised a special envelope featuring the four main colours in a series of flaps, which interleave to encase the card, tied with sheer red ribbon.

You will need ■ teddy bear and flowers rubber stamp ■ graphite black Brilliance™ inkpad ■ brush markers – yellow, orange, spring green, red, blue ■ smooth white card ■ blue, red, yellow and green card ■ white linen-effect folded card 12.5cm (4⁷⁄₈in) square ■ striped printed paper ■ 4 red brads ■ sheer red ribbon

For a softer colour scheme, replace the bright colours with pastel shades of the same colours.

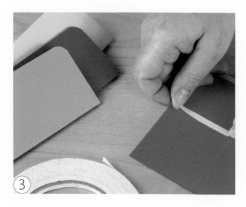

1 Using the inkpad, stamp the image onto smooth white card. Run each brush marker over a plastic lid. Dip a fine paintbrush into clean water, pick up some of the ink and fill in the image and part of the background. Trim the card to 7cm (2¾in) square.

2 Mount the panel on an 8cm (3¼in) square of blue card. Punch a hole in each corner with a 1.5mm (¹⁄₁₆in) holepunch and insert the brads. Cover the folded card with striped paper. Mount the panel on the folded card with adhesive foam pads.

3 Cut a 12.5cm (5in) square of card in blue, red, yellow and green. Score and fold in half. Round off two corners on one side with a corner rounder. Open out one square and lay face down. Apply four lengths of double-sided adhesive tape around one quarter on the unrounded side.

4 Remove the tape backing and place the corner on top of a corner of another square, tucking the edge into the fold. Repeat with the other squares, then stick the last corners together. Glue the ribbon to the envelope back, insert the card and tie in a bow around the interleaved flaps.

Heat Embossing

Heat embossing will give your stamping a new dimension – literally! It is a simple technique achieved in three easy steps: you stamp an image, cover it with embossing powder and heat it. When the powder melts, it forms a plastic skin that raises the lines or surface of the stamped image. It is important to apply the powder to a wet surface, otherwise it will not adhere.

You will need ■ birthday cake rubber stamp ■ lollipop VersaColor™ multicoloured inkpad ■ holographic embossing powder ■ white Liquid Appliqué™ ■ smooth white card 11 x 8cm (4½ x 3¼in) ■ lilac, yellow and apricot card ■ white linen-effect folded card 17 x 11.5cm (6¾ x 4½in) ■ striped printed papers ■ holographic glitter ■ mini star and flower punches ■ purple gingham ribbon

(1)

(2)

(3)

1 Using the inkpad, ink up the stamp so that the tops of the candles are mostly yellow and the base of the cake is purple and blue. Make sure that you move the inkpad in the same direction back and forth to avoid muddying the colours. Stamp onto the smooth white card.

2 Sprinkle a layer of the embossing powder all over the cake. Although pigment ink stays wet for a little while, try to apply the powder straight away. The ink will dry faster if the paper you are using is very absorbent or if the atmosphere you are working in is very warm.

3 Carefully tip the excess powder onto a piece of clean scrap paper. Check that all the image is covered with powder. If any small particles of powder remain around the image, use a fine paintbrush to remove them. Fold the scrap paper over and return the excess powder to the jar.

13 Birthday Celebration

Try embossing a holographic layer over a multicoloured image for a dazzling effect.

You can use this technique with any coloured ink that is suitable for embossing. The holographic embossing powder is transparent, allowing the colours to show through with a touch of sparkle. This cake design also features Liquid Appliqué™, to mimic real icing for an extra-special birthday greeting.

Use a wooden clothes peg to hold the image if it is relatively small, to avoid burning your fingers.

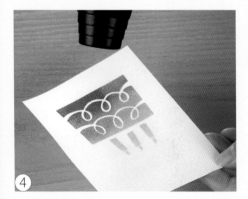
(4)

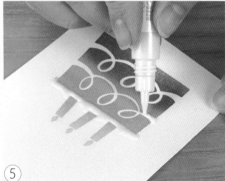
(5)

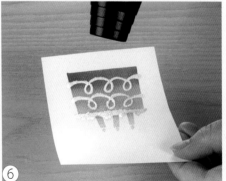
(6)

4 Place the stamped image on a heatproof surface. Point the nozzle of the heat gun towards the image. Turn the power on and move the tool around, keeping at least 2.5cm (1in) away from the image. As soon as one area of powder has melted, move on to the next. Do not overheat.

5 Use white Liquid Appliqué™ to fill in the loops running through the cake and to add a layer of icing on the top. Squeeze the tube gently and hold the nozzle a little way above the image to allow the Liquid Appliqué™ to flow out. White it is still wet, lightly sprinkle with the glitter.

6 Allow the Liquid Appliqué™ to dry and form a hard shell before heating the surface with the heat gun – it will rise and puff up. Avoid re-heating the areas covered in holographic powder and choose a good-quality, fine glitter, which will not melt with the heat.

To Finish

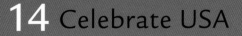

⑦ Attach a ribbon bow to the top of the cake panel. Add some stars and flowers punched from lilac, yellow and apricot card.

⑧ Mark a point 3cm (1¼in) along the folded card top from the right-hand side. Cut from this point to the bottom right-hand corner. Cover the inside back of the folded card with striped paper.

Use a pearlescent embossing powder over ink of the same colour for a softening effect.

This technique has been applied here to two flags, which have been stamped in blue ink and embossed in pearl blue on red card, then cut out and layered to overlap.

You will need ■ American flag rubber stamp ■ royal blue VersaColor™ inkpad ■ pearl blue embossing powder ■ white opaque marker ■ white linen-effect card 7 x 13.5cm (2¾ x 5¼in) ■ red card ■ white linen-effect folded card 17 x 10.5cm (6¾ x 4¼in), fold at the top ■ blue plaid printed paper ■ 2 gold brads

⑨ Glue a 9.5cm (3¾in) wide band of striped paper across the centre of the folded card.

⑩ Trim the two sides of the cake panel so that they converge slightly. Trim the top of the panel at an angle. Mount on a slightly larger piece of lilac card.

⑪ Mount the cake panel on the card with adhesive foam pads.

1 Using the inkpad and embossing powder, stamp and emboss the flag twice on red card. As you cut out both images, be careful not to cut into the embossed line, as this may chip the embossing.

2 Colour in the stars and stripes with the white opaque marker – use different marks such as lines and dots and leave some gaps for a contemporary 'sketchy' effect. Mount both flags onto the piece of white card so that they overlap – one flag flat and the other raised with adhesive foam pads.

3 Mount the flag panel on a slightly larger piece of red card. Cover the bottom two-thirds of the folded card with the plaid printed paper. Draw a stitched line down either side of the paper with the white opaque marker. Punch a hole at the top at each end of the printed paper panel with a 1.5mm (⅟₁₆in) holepunch and insert a brad into each. Mount the flag panel on the card.

> You can use a clear embossing powder instead of the pearl embossing powder for a bolder effect.

15 Mighty Acorns

Experiment with applying several embossing powders over a stamped image.

This technique works best with bold or solid images. You will need to work fairly quickly, applying one powder at a time, so that the ink does not dry out.

The excess embossing powders from the second and third applications will be impure, so don't return them to the original jars.

You will need ■ oak leaves and acorns rubber stamp ■ VersaMark™ inkpad ■ brown VersaColor™ inkpad ■ Metallic Encore™ inkpads – gold, copper ■ embossing powders – pearlescent champagne, copper, orange glitter ■ smooth cream card ■ copper foiled paper ■ brown and tan card ■ gold linen-effect card ■ cream linen-effect folded card 13.5cm (5¼in) square ■ die-cutting tool and leaf die ■ sheer brown ribbon

1 Using the VersaMark™ inkpad, stamp the image onto smooth cream card. Sprinkle small amounts of the champagne embossing powder over selected areas of the wet image. Tip off the excess powder, avoiding the areas not yet covered. Repeat with the copper powder to cover other areas, then the glitter powder. Remove any unwanted specks.

2 Trim the card to 5.5cm (2¼in) square and mount on copper foiled paper. Tear the edges, leaving a narrow border. Mount the panel on a 7cm (2¾in) square of brown card, then a slightly larger piece of gold linen-effect card. Sponge vertical and horizontal lines of brown ink on the folded card using torn strips of paper (see pages 48–51).

3 Die-cut three leaves from tan card (see pages 40–43). Scrunch them up before sponging with the gold and copper inks. Punch holes in the leaves and clip the edges with a 4mm (⅛in) holepunch. Mount the panel on the folded card. Glue the leaves in place. Wrap the ribbon around the front of the card and tie in a knot.

16 Christmas Squares

Use a glitter embossing powder to add festive sparkle to your Christmas cards.

This design features the traditional red and green, using only two brush markers to colour in the images, but other colours could be chosen for a very different result. A glaze applied to areas of the colour adds depth.

Avoid using glitter embossing powders for detailed stamps – as the powder is made up of large particles, you will lose most of the detail.

You will need ■ block of Christmas motifs rubber stamp ■ VersaMark™ inkpad ■ green glitter embossing powder ■ brush markers – red, green ■ clear Sakura Gelly Roll Glaze™ pen ■ smooth white card ■ red and green printed papers ■ white linen-effect folded card 14cm (5½in) square ■ white satin ribbon

1 Using the VersaMark™ inkpad and the green glitter embossing powder, stamp and emboss the block of Christmas motifs onto smooth white card. Trim the card down to 8.5cm (3½in) square.

2 Colour in the images within the squares with the brush markers. Draw over the white, red and green areas slowly with the glaze pen, allowing the glaze to flow out thickly. Leave to dry thoroughly.

3 Mount the panel on a piece of red printed paper 10cm (4in) square, then onto a slightly larger piece of green printed paper. Mount the panel on the folded card. Wrap a length of ribbon around the front left-hand side of the card and tie in a knot.

Shadow Stamps

Shadow stamps are comprised mainly of solid images, such as basic geometric shapes, or arty, brushstroke-effect images and background patterns. They make it easy to build up a backdrop for other images to be stamped over the top. Soft ink tones work best with these stamps so that stronger colour can be applied at a later stage to the main images.

You will need ■ rubber stamps – brushstroke; set of flower heads; block of 4 solid squares ■ tangerine ColorBox Fluid Chalk™ inkpad ■ purple hydrangea VersaMagic Chalk™ inkpad ■ Sakura Gelly Roll Glaze™ pens – orange, black ■ pastel orange textured card 14 x 19cm (5½ x 7½in) ■ 5 pastel orange textured folded cards 7.5cm (3in) square ■ orange paper ■ mini envelope template ■ orange gingham ribbon

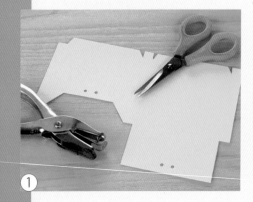

(1)

(2)

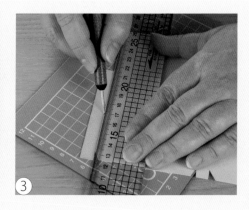

(3)

1 Use the template on page 116 to make your own template from scrap card. Carefully draw around it onto the orange card with a pencil. Mark the holes. Cut out with scissors or use a craft knife and metal ruler, especially if the card is thick. Punch the holes with a 4mm (⅛in) holepunch.

2 Use a corner rounder punch to round off the corners of the flap. Hold the punch in your hand and slide the card into the gap. Guide the corner of the flap into the 'V' shape and squeeze the lever. Repeat the process on the other corner of the flap.

3 Place the card smooth side up on a cutting mat. Use a medium ball embossing tool to score the fold lines – for greater accuracy, mark them out first with a pencil. Use a ruler to guide you as you press down with the tool. Make sure that the scoring is deep enough to create a neat fold.

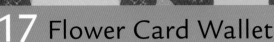

Combine a simple stamped motif with background shadow stamps to create a decorative design.

This approach was used here to adorn a mini wallet housing a handmade set of cards and envelopes, stamped with a coordinating scheme. The cards could have different greetings stamped inside, such as 'Thank You' or 'Missing You'. The stamped design is simple enough so that you can make several of the wallets using the template supplied without difficulty.

You can scale the wallet template up or down on a photocopier to suit the size of the cards/envelopes you want to package.

④

⑤

4 Turn the card textured side up. Using the tangerine inkpad, stamp three brushstrokes, one on each panel, re-inking the rubber between each print. Use the score lines to guide you when lining up the stamp.

5 Select a flower stamp from the set. Using the purple inkpad, stamp two flowers over the brushstroke on the main panel and one over each of the other two brushstrokes, re-inking the stamp between each print. The card texture showing through is part of the effect. Leave to dry.

(6)

6 Use the orange glaze pen to colour in the tiny petals in the centre of each flower. Leave the glaze to dry for a couple of minutes before adding a spot of the black glaze pen in each centre.

(7)

7 Carefully fold the wallet up along the score lines. Apply glue to the side flaps, bring together and hold in place until you have a firm bond. Tuck in the tiny flaps, then repeat the process with the bottom flaps.

(8)

8 Using the tangerine inkpad, stamp the block of squares on the folded cards. Using the purple inkpad, stamp a flower over each square. Repeat Step 6. Use the envelope template to make envelopes from orange paper – the wallet should hold five cards and envelopes. Thread the ribbon through the holes in the wallet and tie in a bow to secure the flap.

18 Home Sweet Home ⋃

Use shadow stamps to create a landscape backdrop for this charming New Home card.

Stamped squares are over-printed with a brushstroke and spots; stamped flowers create the foreground.

You will need ■ rubber stamps – block of rectangles; brushstroke; circle of dots; sketched flowers ■ VersaMagic Chalk™ inkpads – thatched straw, hint of pesto, malted mauve, red brick ■ cream card 12.5cm (5in) square ■ pastel mauve and terracotta textured card ■ sand folded card 13.5cm (5¼in) square ■ die-cutting tool and house die ■ small heart punch ■ cream brad

1 Using the thatched straw inkpad, stamp the block of rectangles onto the cream card. Using the hint of pesto inkpad, stamp the brushstroke over the rectangles just under the halfway point.

2 Using a cotton bud for each colour, add spots of hint of pesto and malted mauve ink over and below the brushstroke. Using the mauve inkpad, stamp the circle of dots over the block of rectangles on the left side. Punch a heart from pastel mauve card for the centre.

3 Die-cut and assemble a house from terracotta and pastel mauve card (see pages 40–43). Add the brad for the door knob and mount the house on the panel with adhesive foam pads. Using the red brick inkpad, stamp some flowers either side of the house. Mount the panel on the folded card.

Mini inkpads are more affordable if you want to have a good range of colours to work with.

19 Sentiments Folder

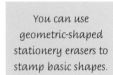

Design and stamp a sheet of decorative paper, with geometric shapes providing a background for stamped flowers.

Here I have cut the printed sheet into panels to create a concertina-style mini folder, which could hold messages or photos of a special occasion.

You will need ■ rubber stamp sets – 'arty' geometric shapes; flowers ■ VersaColor™ inkpads – canary, cyan, pink, fresh green ■ 2 pieces of white linen-effect card 6 x 18cm (2⅜ x 7in) ■ 2 pieces of pink card 6 x 10cm (2⅜ x 4in), 1 piece 6 x 8cm (2⅜ x 3¼in) ■ printed papers ■ 2 pieces of chipboard 6.5cm (2½in) square ■ scraps of yellow, pink and white card ■ punches – large square, small and medium flower ■ pink gingham ribbon

You can use geometric-shaped stationery erasers to stamp basic shapes.

1 Using the canary inkpad, stamp squares at random on the white card strips, leaving room for the other shapes. Repeat with the cyan ink and rectangles. Using the pink ink, stamp a series of circles. Stamp green and pink flowers using two different images.

2 Cut one strip into three. Punch three squares from the other strip. Score a 2cm (¾in) wide flap at each end of the larger pink card pieces. Score a single flap in the smaller pink card. Use the flaps, folded alternate ways, to glue the pink panels to the stamped panels.

3 Cover the chipboard squares with printed paper. Glue ribbon across the centre of one. Attach each end panel of the concertina to a chipboard square. Decorate the pink panels with punched squares and punched flowers. Add punched flowers to the covers.

20 In the Pink

Create a central image by printing a series of small motifs over a stamped grid.

I have used chalk inks in this design, which mimic the effect of chalk pastels, for a soft, dusty finish. A hint of a black outline was drawn freehand over the flowers to add definition.

Stamp several spare pieces of card so that you can practise your freehand drawing before tackling the real thing.

You will need ■ rubber stamps – block of nine squares; sketched flowers and butterflies ■ ColorBox Fluid Chalk™ inkpads – ice blue, Prussian blue, orchid pastel, dark peony ■ black Sakura Gelly Roll Glaze™ pen ■ pale turquoise and turquoise textured card ■ pale pink linen-effect folded card 14cm (5½in) square ■ heart button ■ pink embroidery thread

1 Using the ice blue inkpad, stamp the block of squares onto the textured side of the pale turquoise card. Using the Prussian blue inkpad, stamp a flower and a butterfly alternately in the squares, leaving the central one blank.

2 Using cotton buds, sponge orchid pastel, dark peony and Prussian blue ink over the stamped motifs. Gently brush and dab the cotton buds across the card surface to build up the colour gradually.

3 Use the glaze pen to trace over parts of the images and to add a frame to each alternate square. Trim the card to 8.5cm (3½in) square. Mount onto a slightly larger piece of turquoise card. Mount the panel on the folded card with adhesive foam pads. Thread the embroidery thread through the holes of the button – the thread can be split into strands and as many strands used as will fill the buttonholes attractively. Tie in a knot on the front. Glue the button to the central square of the panel with Hi-Tack Glue™.

Clear Stamps

Made from polymer rather than rubber, clear stamps have revolutionized stamping. You simply mount a die on a clear acrylic block, ink it up and stamp. Repeat patterns and fitting an image into a given space are made so much easier by being able to see exactly where you are stamping through the block. Storage is trouble-free too, as only one block is required and the stamp dies can be stored in an expanding wallet.

You will need ■ wine bottle and glasses, cheese and cutlery set of clear stamps ■ clear acrylic block ■ graphite black Brilliance™ inkpad ■ VersaMark™ inkpad ■ silver pen ■ turquoise and pale turquoise card ■ sea green printed paper ■ silver linen-effect card ■ die-cutting tool and circular frame and circle dies ■ 5cm (2in) square punch ■ black ribbon

1 Remove the wine bottle stamp die from the storage base and press it down on the acrylic block. There should not be any parts of the die overhanging the block, so always use one that is bigger than the die. Check that the die is secure on the block.

2 Cut a piece of turquoise card 19 x 9cm (7½ x 3½in). Stick a narrow strip of the printed paper along the bottom of the card. Using the black inkpad, stamp the bottle, then the wine glasses slightly overlapping the strip. Clean the dies and return them to the storage base as you use them.

3 Clean the block if necessary and place the cheese die on it. Using the VersaMark™ inkpad, stamp the cheese at random all over the turquoise card above the bottles and glasses, altering the angle for each print to create an interesting pattern.

21 Cheese and Wine Party

Try using clear stamps to tackle a tricky Layout.

Knowing where to stamp the various elements in this party invitation, such as the bottle, glasses and cutlery, would have been difficult using ordinary rubber stamps. Here, I have devised the composition to allow space in the centre for the relevant details to be added. The cheese motif could be changed to relate to a different occasion or the colour scheme tied in to a seasonal event.

Instead of printing separately, you can arrange the bottle and glasses in position on the block to print them in one go.

(4)

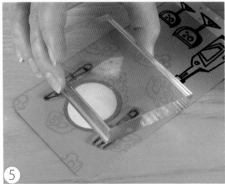

(5)

(6)

4 Die-cut a circular frame from the silver card and a same-size or slightly smaller circle from pale turquoise card (see pages 40–43). Stick the circle in the centre of the panel towards the top and add the frame to create a plate.

5 You may want to use parts of a die separately, as with this cutlery. Cut through the polymer to separate. Make sure that they are clean, then place, stamping surface down, either side of the plate. Adjust the positioning. Gradually lower the block on top to pick up the dies. Use the black inkpad to stamp.

6 Using the black inkpad, stamp the cheese on turquoise card and cut out. Punch a large square from the printed paper and cut away a triangular section to create a napkin. Glue the napkin to the plate and add the cheese with adhesive foam pads.

7 Use the silver pen to colour in some sections of the cutlery, bottle and glasses. Focus on details such as the bubbles in the bottle and glasses, the handles of the knife and fork and the wine label.

8 Round off the two top corners of the panel with a corner rounder punch. Mount onto a slightly larger piece of pale turquoise card. Punch two holes 2cm (¾in) apart at the top of the panel with a 1.5mm (¹⁄₁₆in) holepunch. Thread ribbon through both holes from the back to the front and tie in a bow.

Take a fun motif from your invitaton, such as this wedge of cheese, and feature it on other party accessories such as place cards.

Combine repeat images from different dies to create unique, fun designs.

Here, a baby has been stamped twice, then a teddy bear hat stamped on each baby's head to make cute identical twins.

You will need ■ baby and hats, hearts, hugs and kisses set of clear stamps ■ clear acrylic block ■ Mediterranean blue Brilliance™ inkpad ■ white Sakura Soufflé™ pen ■ pale blue and blue card ■ blue striped printed paper ■ white linen-effect folded card 16.5 x 11cm (6½ x 4½in), fold at the top ■ silver linen-effect card ■ die-cutting tool and rattle die ■ white sheer ribbon

1 Using the inkpad, stamp the baby twice, side by side, onto pale blue card. Stamp a teddy bear hat over each head. Add some hearts, hugs and kisses between the babies.

2 Dip a paintbrush into clean water, pick up some ink from the blue inkpad and use to add shading to the babies, teddy bear hats, hearts and background. Leave to dry, then add white highlights with the white pen – it turns from clear to white as it dries.

3 Trim the card to 7 x 12.5cm (2¾ x 5in). Mount on a slightly larger piece of blue card. Glue a 10.5cm (4¼in) wide band of striped paper to the folded card centre. Glue a narrow silver card strip either side. Mount the panel on the card with adhesive foam pads. Die-cut two silver rattles, keeping only the star cutout of one. Glue a tiny piece of pale blue card behind the star aperture of the other. Tie ribbon around the handle. Mount on the card with adhesive foam pads. Add the star cutouts.

Store your clear stamps in a clean, dust-free environment so that they do not lose their cling.

Since you can see exactly where to stamp each element, creating elaborate flower arrangements could not be easier with clear stamps.

Start by stamping the larger elements – the open roses in this case – and progress to the foliage and tiny blooms.

You will need ■ flowers and foliage set of clear stamps ■ clear acrylic block ■ brush makers – red, purple, pink, spring green, green ■ white linen-effect folded card 14.5cm (5¾in) square ■ white linen-effect card 4.5 x 8cm (1¾ x 3¼in) ■ silver card ■ purple paper ■ die-cutting tool and horseshoe and number dies ■ mini flowers corner punch ■ white sheer ribbon ■ holographic glitter glue

Use a clear alphabet set to stamp individual decorative letters on a row of tags.

As these tags are die-cut, the stamping was done after the cutting. I used clear shadow stamps to print background blocks behind the letters, to add depth to the tags.

You will need ■ clear stamp sets – patterned backgrounds; flowery capital letters ■ pink petunia VersaMagic™ inkpad ■ brown VersaColor™ inkpad ■ brown, pale pink and olive green card ■ olive green folded card 17 x 10cm (6¾ x 4in), fold at the top ■ plaid printed paper ■ die-cutting tool and scallop-shaped tag and belt buckle dies ■ 5 pink brads ■ pink ribbon ■ small and medium flower punches

If you don't have a die-cutting system, you could use stickers for the horseshoes and numbers.

1 Ink up the die of the two roses with the red brush marker and stamp onto the folded card. Stamp the smaller roses, one either side, the rosebuds and then the smaller flowers and foliage. Use a paintbrush and clean water to wash over the stamped lines and dilute the colours to fill the open spaces within and around the flowers and foliage.

2 Mount the piece of white card on a slightly larger piece of silver card. Die-cut two horseshoes and the numbers 2 and 5 from silver card (see pages 40–43). Glue to the panel. Punch holes around the edge of each horseshoe with a 1.5mm (¹⁄₁₆in) holepunch.

3 Thread a length of the ribbon in and out through the holes and between the horseshoes. Secure the ends of the ribbon to the back of the panel. Add tiny flowers punched from purple paper and mount the panel on the card with adhesive foam pads. Highlight the flowers with the glitter glue.

1 Die-cut four tags from brown card and four slightly smaller tags from pink card (see pages 40–43). Using the pink inkpad, stamp a different background on each of the pink tags. Using the brown inkpad, stamp the letter 'A' onto two tags and the letter 'N' onto the other two tags to spell out 'Anna'.

Instead of a name, you can use the alphabet stamps to spell out 'Hello', 'Smile' or 'Thanks' on the tags.

2 Glue the pink tags to the brown tags, aligning the holes. Punch a hole in each letter flower centre with a 1.5mm (¹⁄₁₆in) holepunch and insert a brad. Tie ribbon to each tag. Punch a small and medium flower from olive green and brown card. Secure together with a brad.

3 Cover the lower three-quarters of the folded card front with a 7cm (2¾in) wide band of the plaid paper. Die-cut a buckle from olive green card. Slip the buckle onto a 1cm (³⁄₈in) wide strip of brown card and stick along the top of the paper. Mount the tags and flower with adhesive foam pads.

Die-Cuts & Punches

Most stampers have a collection of punches that they use mainly for embellishing. In this section, you will see how you can go one step further by using die-cutting systems in conjunction with both punches and stamps. You can dress up your die-cuts by stamping over them or use die-cuts together with a stamped image to create an entire design. Either way, the results are impressive. Always read the manufacturer's operating instructions carefully before using any die-cutting system.

You will need ■ hibiscus flower and leaf rubber stamp ■ black StazOn™ inkpad ■ limone VersaColor™ inkpad ■ pale orange linen-effect card ■ orange and brown plaid printed paper ■ scraps of card – brown, tan, lime green, pale grey, grey, pale blue, pale orange, orange ■ Sakura Gelly Roll Glaze™ pens – red, orange ■ lime green Sakura Soufflé™ pen ■ Sissix™ die-cutting tool and Original Dies 38-1138 Album Cover, 38-1139 Album Page Inserts ■ Quickutz™ die-cutting tool and Dies KS-0286 Suitcase, KS-0365 Camera, KS- 0165 Shirt, RS-0026 Flip-Flops ■ small flower punch ■ Japanese paper cord ■ raffia ■ sandpaper

(1)

(2)

(3)

1 Using the Sizzix™ tool, cut two covers from pale orange card and page inserts from plaid paper: place card or paper larger than the die on the cutting pad; place the die, cutting side down, on top and slide the pad below the press; push the handle down. Slide the pad back and forward.

2 Rub random areas of both album covers with sandpaper to distress. Using the black inkpad, stamp the hibiscus image onto the front cover. Start from one side and continue re-inking and stamping until you have stamped evenly all over the cover. Repeat with the back cover. Clean the stamp.

3 Use the glaze pens to colour in the flowers and the Soufflé™ pen for the leaves. Both types of pen contain ink that requires a few minutes to dry, so colour in a small section at a time.

Use a clever combination of die-cuts and stamps to create a unique front cover for a mini travel journal.

A bold, exotic flower motif stamped across the album covers to create an all-over pattern makes a lively backdrop for some die-cut vacation essentials, such as a smart suitcase complete with luggage label and some flower-trimmed flip-flops. I made extra use here of the same stamp but with a different-coloured ink to decorate the shirt die-cut. A similar cover design could be easily themed for a party, birth or graduation booklet.

Before using the Quickutz™ die-cutting tool, make sure that the dies you want to use have been covered with the ejection foam supplied with the die-cutting system.

(4)

(5)

4 Using the Quickutz™ tool, die-cut the main suitcase and luggage label, shirt, camera and flip-flops from the appropriate card: slide a die, cutting side down, between the pressure plates; slide card between the die and bottom plate; squeeze the handles until you hear clicking, then release.

5 Using the lime green inkpad, ink up the stamp carefully. Check that there is ink all over the rubber, then stamp onto the shirt front. Continue re-inking and stamping until you have covered the whole of the shirt front.

(6)

6 Leave the ink to dry. Using a glue stick, glue the shirt front to the shirt back.

(7)

7 Assemble the die-cut pieces for the camera, suitcase and flip-flops and glue together in the same way. For smaller items, such as the suitcase corners, use PVA (white) glue applied with a cocktail stick or from a glue dispenser with a fine nozzle. Punch two flowers from orange card and glue to the flip-flops. Thread the ends of a short length of cord through the holes in the camera and knot.

(8)

8 Place the page inserts between the album covers and secure together with lengths of raffia threaded through the holes and tied in a bow at the front. Attach the die-cuts to the cover with adhesive foam pads. Twist the camera strap and attach to the cover with PVA (white) glue.

26 Hee–Haw!

Use a die-cutting system to create an embellished frame for a stamped picture.

This card would be great as a good luck greeting for a horse lover or line-dancing enthusiast!

You will need ▪ rubber stamps – cowboy chick; swirling star ▪ graphite black Brilliance™ inkpad ▪ midnight blue StazOn™ inkpad ▪ colouring pencils ▪ white linen-effect card ▪ printed papers – denim-effect, red plaid ▪ white linen-effect folded card 14cm (5½in) square ▪ silver card ▪ scraps of card – tan, brown, lime green, red, blue ▪ die-cutting tool and large frame, horseshoe, boot, hat and cacti dies ▪ small star punch

1 Die-cut a large frame from the white card. Place the central panel on scrap card. Using the black inkpad, stamp the chick onto the central panel. Colour in the design with colouring pencils.

2 Cover a piece of the white card larger than the frame die with denim-effect paper. Die-cut the frame from the covered card. Using the blue inkpad, stamp the swirling star stamp at random over the frame.

3 Cover the folded card with plaid paper. Mount the frame onto the card with adhesive pads. Glue the stamped panel inside the frame. Die-cut the horseshoe, boot, hat and cacti from the coloured card and glue to the frame. Punch a star from red, white and blue card and attach to the frame with adhesive foam pads.

Keep leftover scraps of paper for die-cutting and punching.

27 Birthday Cake

Use die-cut motifs as the main focus of the design, cutting the various elements from different coloured card and paper.

Stamping is then used here to add decorative interest.

You will need ■ heart, star and spiral rubber stamp ■ pearlescent coral Brilliance™ inkpad ■ card – peach, pink ■ polka-dot printed paper ■ orange folded card 12cm (4¾in) square ■ die-cutting tool and birthday cake with candles and cupcake with cherry dies ■ narrow red and white ribbon ■ holographic glitter glue

Change the background paper and card to create your own design.

1 Die-cut a birthday cake and cupcake and cherry from peach card. Using the coral inkpad, stamp the motif all over the large cake and parts of the cupcake. Using a wet paintbrush, pick up ink from the edge of the inkpad and colour in.

2 Die-cut another birthday cake from pink card and one from polka-dot paper. Use the detail lines on the cakes as a guide to cut out the plate from the pink cake and icing from the polka-dot cake. Stick each piece over its corresponding area on the peach cake. Die-cut three candles from pink and peach card. Cut away the flames from the pink candles. Glue to the peach candles. Glue to the cake.

3 Cut a 10.5cm (4¼in) peach card square. Cut pink card 4 x 9.5cm (1½ x 3¾in). Mount the pink card on the upper part of the peach card, then glue polka-dot paper 6 x 9.5cm (2⅜ x 3¾in) to the lower part of the peach card, slightly overlapping the pink card. Glue ribbon across the join, adding a bow. Mount on the folded card. Mount the cake on the panel. Die-cut a second pink cupcake and cherry. Assemble the stamped peach and pink die-cuts of the cupcakes and cherries. Mount on the card with adhesive foam pads. Add highlights with glitter glue.

28 Coloured Tags

Make a rainbow tag learning tool, decorated with die-cuts, punches and embellishments.

For safety, ensure that any small items are securely stuck down.

You can create other learning tools such as numbers or letters of the alphabet.

You will need ■ rubber stamps – Stampendous H197 Snail Fluffles, F133 Flower Fluffles; Penny Black 1758E Garden Buggy, 2354F Hedgy Flavor; Azadi Earles F483 Jack in the Box, G970 Smiling Sun ■ VersaColor™ inkpads – green, imperial blue, violet, rose red, orange, marigold ■ clear embossing powder ■ Plaid Clear Dimensional Magic™ ■ white card ■ textured card – green, blue, purple, red, orange, yellow ■ die-cutting tool and large tag, comb, leaf, grass, truck, crayon, gift, balloon, cap, strawberry, ice cream, duck and key dies ■ Punches – bear, heart, spiral, butterfly, star ■ embellishments – buttons, red foam flower, wooden ladybird, string ■ book ring ■ ribbon – green, blue, purple, red, orange, yellow

1 Stamp onto white card: Snail Fluffles in green ink, Flower Fluffles in blue, Garden Buggy in violet, Jack in the Box in red, Hedgy Flavor in orange and Smiling Sun in yellow. Heat emboss with clear embossing powder (see pages 28–31). Colour in by picking up a little of the appropriate ink with a wet paintbrush. Trim down all the images. Use a corner rounder to round off the corners.

2 Die-cut a tag from each textured card colour. Die-cut a comb, leaves and grass from green card, truck and crayon from blue card, gift and balloon from purple card, cap and strawberry from red card, ice cream from orange card and duck and key from yellow card. Punch a bear and heart from blue card, a spiral from purple card, hearts from red card, butterflies from orange card and stars from yellow card.

3 Gather together all the items for each tag. Arrange the stamped panel, die-cuts and punched shapes and embellishments on each tag, including a length of string for the balloon, and stick in place with the appropriate glue. Cover the leaves and truck with a coat of the Dimensional Magic™. Leave to dry. Thread the tags onto the book ring and tie on a length of ribbon in each colour.

Masking

The word masking means to cover or hide, and in rubber stamping the technique of masking is used to bring elements of a design to the forefront by covering the main image with a mask, then stamping over it with another image. You can use masking to compose a naturalistic group image from a repeated print of a single motif, or for stamping an image within a frame or to create a scene. This is a versatile technique and the results are very effective.

You will need ■ ghouls rubber stamp ■ cherry pink StazOn™ inkpad ■ graphite black Brilliance™ inkpad ■ lime pearlescent paint ■ Liquid Applique™ – white, grey ■ Plaid Clear Dimensional Magic™ ■ JudiKins Masking Paper™ ■ white card 13.5cm (5¼in) square ■ black glossy card ■ orange folded card 15cm (6in) square ■ die-cutting tool and spider and bat dies ■ wiggly eyes ■ Superglue

1 Carefully unroll the masking paper and cut off a section large enough for the mask. Using the pink inkpad, ink the stamp up carefully. Check that there is ink all over the rubber, then stamp onto the masking paper. Leave the ink to dry while you clean the rubber stamp.

2 Using small scissors, cut around the image, cutting into the stamped line to avoid the halo effect that can occur when stamping over an edge. Using the black inkpad, stamp onto the white card to the left of centre. Leave to dry, then place the mask over the image.

3 Re-ink the stamp and make a second print of the motif onto the white card, stamping the second ghoul partly over the mask. When the mask is removed, the first ghoul will be in the foreground and the second ghoul will appear to be peering cheekily over his shoulder.

Use masking to make one motif appear behind the other with a single stamp.

Any paper can be used to make a mask, but the thinner it is, the better, so use a self-adhesive note or masking paper for optimum results. Use permanent ink in a contrasting colour for stamping your mask so that you can clearly see where you have placed it and avoid activating the ink on the edge of the mask. For added fun and to emphasize the Halloween theme, I have used a bold lime pearlescent colour to halo the ghouls. Liquid Appliqué™ is ideal for creating the webs and to add dimension to the ghouls.

Rather than waiting for the Liquid Appliqué™ to dry, you can heat it straight after application while it is still wet, but the results are less predictable.

(4)

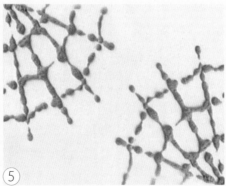

(5)

(6)

4 Apply lime green pearlescent paint around the ghouls and paint the eyes and mouths. Leave to dry. Squeeze white Liquid Appliqué™ in random patches over both ghouls. Using a heat gun, apply heat to the Liquid Appliqué™, which will then rise and puff up.

5 Use the grey Liquid Appliqué™ to draw a web in the two top and the bottom right-hand corners of the panel. Leave to dry so that a hard shell forms. Paint over the eyes and teeth of both ghouls with the Dimensional Magic™.

6 Die-cut the spider and two bats from black glossy card. Attach wiggly eyes to the spider with Superglue, then mount onto the main panel with adhesive foam pads. To finish, mount the main panel on black glossy card, then onto orange folded card.

30 Caught Out

Mask an image with an aperture mask,
then stamp a design through the aperture.

Here I have used two masks to stamp a motif within a
frame and to build up a series of overlapping images.

After spending the time cutting out
masks, don't throw them away!
Instead, catalogue and store them
in a ring binder attached to plastic
sleeves for future use.

You will need

■ rubber stamps – filmstrip
frame; cat and flowerpot
■ cherry pink StazOn™ inkpad
■ graphite black Brilliance™
inkpad ■ felt-tip pens
■ Plaid Clear Dimensional
Magic™ ■ JudiKins Masking
Paper™ ■ white and black
card ■ lilac linen-effect folded
card 7.5 x 16cm (3 x 6¼in)
■ filmstrip border punch

①

②

1 Using the pink inkpad, stamp
the filmstrip frame twice onto
masking paper. Cut out the
centre to create an aperture. Cut
around the edge of the other
frame. Using the black inkpad,
stamp one filmstrip frame onto
white card. Leave to dry, then
place the mask over the frame.
Then stamp the image through
the aperture. Leave to dry.

2 Cover the filmstrip frame with the
solid frame mask. Stamp another
filmstrip frame overlapping the
first. Leaving that mask in place,
cover the second frame with the
aperture mask and stamp the
image through the frame but
positioned slightly differently.
Repeat again. Colour in with
felt-tip pens and cut out as a
single piece.

3 Stamp the image onto the right-
hand end of white card
6.5 x 14.5cm (2½ x 5¾in) and
colour in. Punch the left-hand
side of the panel with the border
punch, attaching a small piece of
black card to the reverse. Paint the
flowers with Dimensional Magic™.
Mount the panel on the folded
card. Mount the filmstrip sequence
with adhesive foam pads.

31 Bumblebee Blooms

Use the masking technique to combine and overlap different stamped images, creating a convincing illusion of depth.

This card would suit a summer birthday celebration.

If you are using a lot of masks, number them in the order in which they are to be used to remind yourself of the sequence.

You will need ■ clear stamp sets – 3 different flower heads, stems, large leaf, small leaf, butterfly, bumblebee ■ clear acrylic block ■ cherry pink StazOn™ inkpad ■ saddle brown StazOn™ inkpad ■ decorating chalks ■ JudiKins Masking Paper™ ■ cream parchment card 15 x 10cm (6 x 4in) ■ cream linen-effect folded card 18 x 13cm (7 x 5in) ■ red printed paper ■ lime green card ■ holographic glitter glue ■ 2 bumble bee stickers

1 Using the pink inkpad, stamp the three flower heads, long stem and large leaf onto masking paper and cut out. Using the brown inkpad, stamp the largest bloom centrally onto the cream parchment card. Cover with the corresponding mask and stamp the second bloom to overlap on the left-hand side. Stamp the third bloom as shown.

2 Cover all flowers with masks, then use the brown inkpad to stamp the stems in position. Mask the long stem below the left-hand bloom and stamp the large leaf across it. Stamp the small leaf, butterfly and bumblebee and use the chalks to colour in the design.

3 Cover about three-quarters of the front panel of the folded card with red paper. Mount the flower panel on a slightly larger piece of lime green card, then onto the folded card. Embellish with the glitter glue and bumble bee stickers.

32 Ahoy There!

By masking only part of an image, you can use the masking technique to create foreground and background detailing.

In this design, I masked just the hulls of the boats in order to stamp the wave so that it appears in the background.

You will need ■ boat, wave and seagulls set of clear stamps ■ clear acrylic block ■ cherry pink StazOn™ inkpad ■ teal blue StazOn™ inkpad ■ teal blue felt-tip pen ■ Plaid Clear Dimensional Magic™ ■ white card ■ pale and dark teal blue card ■ white linen-effect folded card 9 x 16.5cm (3½ x 6½in) ■ 6 white eyelets ■ 26-gauge turquoise blue wire ■ white beads

When stamping three motifs in a row, it is much easier to achieve an even positioning if you stamp the central one first, measuring and marking the position in pencil.

1 Using the pink inkpad, stamp the boat stamp three times onto masking paper. Cut out the three hulls only, disregarding the remainder. Using the teal blue inkpad, stamp three boats onto white card. Cover the three hulls with the three masks and stamp the wave across them. Stamp seagulls in the sky above.

2 Run the teal blue pen over a plastic lid or piece of foil. Pick up the colour with a wet paintbrush and apply shades across the boats, sky and wave. Cover sections of the boats and the crest of the wave with Dimensional Magic™. Mount the panel on a piece of pale teal blue card. Using a 1.5mm (¹⁄₁₆in) holepunch, punch two holes in each hull and set eyelets in place (see page 101).

3 Punch two holes in each end of the panel below the wave. Thread a length of the wire with the beads, then twist and curl it. Thread either end through one hole and out the other, then twist with a cocktail stick to secure. Cover part of the folded card with torn dark teal blue card. Mount the panel centrally on top with adhesive foam pads.

Sponging

A sponge applies colour to a surface in a unique way. Once you have learned how to control the technique, you can use sponging to apply and blend soft layers of colour. Sponging is very useful for filling in spaces around stamped images and for creating artistic backgrounds such as skies or sunsets. Try experimenting with different types of sponges and other soft materials such as clingfilm to achieve a variety of effects.

You will need ■ dragonfly rubber stamp ■ VersaMark™ inkpad ■ VersaColor™ inkpads – canary, marigold, paprika, brown ■ clear embossing powder ■ pale mango card 20cm (8in) square ■ holographic glitter glue

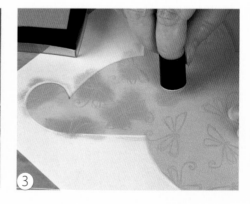

1 Use the template on page 116 to make your own template from scrap card. Draw around it onto the mango card with a pencil and cut out. Using the VersaMark™ inkpad and embossing powder, stamp and heat emboss dragonflies at random all over the card (see pages 28–31).

2 Place the card on scrap paper. Press a sponge dauber gently onto the yellow inkpad. See how much ink you have picked up by pressing the sponge down onto scrap paper. The degree of pressure controls the flow of ink. Sponge random patches all over the background and dragonflies.

3 Repeat the sponging process with the marigold orange ink. Fill in some of the gaps between the yellow patches. Use the sponge dauber to blend the colours together where they meet.

33 Dragonfly Box

Learn how to sponge ink over embossed images to create an effect that resembles batik.

The dragonflies on this elegant gift box have been stamped using a clear inkpad and embossed with clear embossing powder. This allows the colour of the card to show through under the embossing once you start to sponge ink across the surface. With a touch of holographic glitter added to the wings, the dragonflies shimmer over the box.

If you intend to sponge ink over an embossed image, avoid using glitter embossing powders, otherwise the sponge may snag on the glitter.

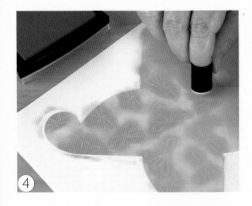

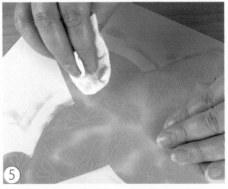

4 To finish the process, sponge some paprika ink in the remaining gaps. If you need to do some further blending, use a clean sponge dauber to avoid applying too much of the darker tone. The ink should remain wet enough for you to do this.

5 Use a piece of kitchen paper to remove any ink left on the embossed lines – this is necessary, as the ink will not dry naturally, since it cannot be absorbed. As you remove the ink, the dragonflies will become more visible. The base card colour will show through the lines.

6 Using a wet paintbrush, pick up ink from the brown inkpad and colour in the dragonflies' wings. When dry, apply the glitter glue. Leave to dry thoroughly. Turn the card over and score the fold lines with a medium ball embossing tool. Gently fold over the flaps and slot together.

34 Poppy Field

Use sponges to blend bands of colours into a scenic backdrop.

This design features a sponged sunset-style background, which provides the perfect summery setting for a picturesque rural landscape abloom with poppies – an ideal, relaxing image to celebrate retirement.

You will need ■ landscape with poppies rubber stamp ■ VersaColor™ inkpads – canary, orange, scarlet ■ graphite black Brilliance™ inkpad ■ VersaMark™ inkpad ■ cream pearlescent card 7 x 5cm (2¾ x 2in) ■ mango card 13 x 10cm (5 x 4in) ■ pale pink vellum ■ red card ■ multi-shaded orange and red fibres

Instead of using a standard envelope, you could present the tag in a small pocket made from vellum.

1 Using a sponge dauber, apply a narrow band of yellow ink to the top of the cream card, then a band of orange and finally scarlet on the bottom part of the card. Leave to dry.

2 Using the black inkpad, stamp the landscape onto the sponged background. Use a wet paintbrush to pick up ink from the inkpads to colour in the poppies, house and trees. Cut out the image, leaving a narrow border.

3 Using the VersaMark™ inkpad, stamp the landscape at random over the mango card. Trim the corners and cut an aperture 7 x 5cm (2¾in x 2in) to one side. Mount torn vellum halfway across the aperture with a glue stick. Mount on a slightly larger piece of red card, trimming the corners. Mount the landscape in the aperture. Punch a hole with a 6mm (¼in) holepunch, thread with fibres and tie in a knot.

35 Blue Flowers

Experiment with using a ball of clingfilm to apply ink to create a unique background.

As the surface of the clingfilm ball is not flat, it will leave a pattern behind with each print. The pearlescent colours used here blend particularly well.

You will need ■ flowers and foliage rubber stamp ■ peacock Brilliance™ inkpad ■ brilliant blue Mica Magic™ inkpad ■ clingfilm ■ white linen-effect card 12 x 7cm (4¾ x 2¾in) ■ blue card ■ pale green linen-effect folded card 16 x 11cm (6¼ x 4½in) ■ pale green linen-effect card ■ tag punch ■ royal blue ribbon ■ holographic glitter glue

1 Roll a length of clingfilm into a loose ball shape. Dab across the two greens on the Brilliance™ inkpad to pick up the ink and gently press onto the white card. Repeat until the whole card is covered, adding some blue ink down the sides and in the corners.

2 Using the blue inkpad, stamp the image onto the sponged card. Use a wet paintbrush to pick up some ink from the pad and paint a shadow behind the flower. Mount the panel on a slightly larger piece of blue card. Clean the rubber and use the blue Brilliance™ inkpad to stamp the flower image across the folded card.

3 Punch a tag from the pale green card and use both inkpads to stamp parts of the image over it. Press the edges of the tag onto the blue inkpad. Punch a hole in the tag with a 4mm (⅛in) holepunch and thread with ribbon. Mount the panel on the card. Add the tag with adhesive foam pads. Highlight the flowers and leaves with the glitter glue.

As this technique can be a little messy, wear protective gloves to keep your hands clean.

Combine sponging with masking (see pages 44–47) to create an interesting all-over pattern for a background.

The bubbles here have been die-cut from masking paper so that they adhere to the surface while the ink is sponged around. Further sponging has been used to fill the space around the mouse and to apply delicate tones to the floating bubbles, which are raised to add to the effect.

You will need ■ mouse on a champagne cork rubber stamp ■ VersaColor™ inkpads – pink, canary, cyan ■ graphite black Brilliance™ inkpad ■ brush markers – green, brown, black, pink ■ JudiKins Masking Paper™ ■ smooth white card ■ pink pearlescent folded card 21 x 10cm (8¼ x 4in) ■ pale yellow, pale pink and pale green card ■ die-cutting tool and small, medium and large bubbles; champagne bottle and cork dies ■ holographic glitter glue

> *Always use a clean sponge for applying pale inks such as white and yellow, as they easily become contaminated both on the sponge and inkpad.*

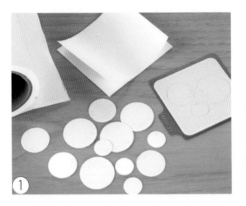

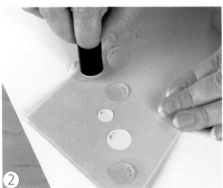

1 Stick masking paper to white card. Die-cut bubbles in each size (see pages 40–43). On the folded card, mark a point 3cm (1⅛in) from the top and 2.5cm (1in) in from the right-hand side on the base. Cut from the top left-hand corner to the first mark. Repeat with the first and second marks.

2 Remove the layer of masking paper from the die-cut bubbles. Place the bubbles on the top portion of the folded card and sponge pink ink over the edges of the masks. Lift the masks, place them further down and sponge again. Repeat until the whole front is covered in bubbles.

3 Using the black inkpad, stamp the mouse onto white card. Colour in with the brush markers diluted with water. Trim the card to angle the sides. Sponge pink ink onto the background. Mount on a slightly larger piece of yellow card, then on the folded card with adhesive foam pads.

4 Sponge yellow, blue and pink ink over spare bubbles. Die-cut and assemble a champagne bottle from yellow, pink and green card. Add sponged highlights. Arrange and mount the bubbles and bottle on the card with adhesive foam pads. Add glitter glue to the bubbles, mouse and bottle.

Vellum

Vellum can offer a great deal more than just an additional surface to stamp on. Available in a variety of thicknesses, colours and printed patterns, it can be used to complement all kinds of stamped images. If stamping on vellum, however, you must take into account its smooth and slightly slippery surface. You must also use inks that will dry on its non-porous surface, or emboss the image.

You will need ■ hearts, bouquet and champagne glasses set of rubber stamps ■ rocket red Brilliance™ inkpad ■ plain vellum ■ red and green card ■ silver linen-effect card ■ white textured card 18 x 21cm (7 x 8¼in) ■ 2 pieces of pearl embossed printed paper 18 x 8cm (7 x 3¼in) ■ large square frame punch ■ die-cutting tool and heart tag and rosebud dies ■ white satin ribbon

(1)

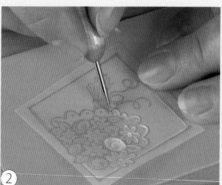

(2)

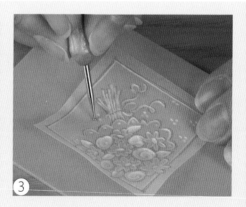

(3)

1 Using the inkpad, stamp the hearts, bouquet and champagne glasses twice on vellum. Rub the end of a fine ball embossing tool in the palm of your hand to pick up oil from your skin so that it will glide more easily over the surface of the vellum.

2 Place one of the bouquet images right side down on a foam mat. Draw the embossing tool over the vellum, pressing down gently to produce a white mark. In this way, fill in the flowers, stems, ribbon and frill.

3 Draw spots in the background around the bouquet. Repeat with the second bouquet, but only emboss the frill and flowers. Prepare the hearts and glasses in the same way, but fill in the backgrounds using crosses around the hearts and wavy lines around the glasses. Set aside.

37 Red Rosebuds

Use stamping and embossing on vellum to build up delicate layers.

Each of the three wedding images used on this tri-fold card have been stamped twice so that elements can be cut away from one set and used for layering the other. This results in giving the flowers, hearts and glasses an intriguing three-dimensional appearance. Mounting the vellum squares on open frames allows more light to pass through them. The overall effect is highly decorative yet subtle.

Allow a little longer for the ink to dry on vellum than on ordinary card. If necessary, use a heat gun to speed up the process.

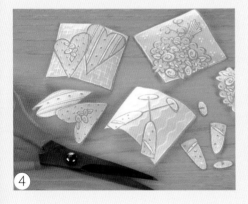

4 Cut out the overlapping hearts, glasses tops and bases and bouquet flowers and frill carefully from the other images. Apply tiny dots of Hi-Tack Glue™ to the edges of the bouquet and frill. Stick directly on top of the other bouquet. Repeat with the glasses and hearts.

5 Punch three square frames from red card. Cut out the frames using scissors, as they remain attached to the card. Trim off the notches remaining on the sides of the punched frames.

6 Mount the vellum squares on the frames – apply tiny dots of Hi-Tack Glue™ to the corners of the vellum, then press down until the glue begins to set. Die-cut a heart tag from the silver card and the parts for three red rosebuds from red and green card (see pages 40–43), then assemble.

To Finish

⑦ Score the white textured card 6cm (2¼in) and 13.5cm (5¼in) from the left-hand side to create three panels. Fold the card into a 'Z'.

⑧ Tear down one side of each piece of the pearl embossed paper. Mount both pieces on the folded card, leaving a 1cm (⅜in) gap between the untorn edges on the central panel of the card.

⑨ Mount the three rosebuds overlapping the torn edge of the paper on the left-hand panel of the card.

⑩ Mount the three framed vellum squares overlapping the torn edge of the paper on the right-hand panel.

⑪ Thread the heart tag onto the ribbon, wrap around the central panel and tie in a bow.

38 Polar Fun

Use embossing on vellum to create wintry scenes and textured effects.

In this novel Christmas design, embossing perfectly captures the essence of a snowy night under the light of a frosty moon, as well as adding texture to the bears' fur.

You will need ■ polar bears and sleigh rubber stamp ■ Mediterranean blue Brilliance™ inkpad ■ plain vellum 11 x 14.5cm (4½ x 5¾in) ■ blue folded card 14.5 x 11cm (5¾ x 4½in), fold at the top ■ white card ■ small circle punch ■ 2 white eyelets

1 Using the blue inkpad, stamp the image onto the vellum. Make sure that the ink is thoroughly dry before turning the vellum over and placing it on a foam mat.

2 Using a fine ball embossing tool, draw fur on all four bears, a row of mountains just above the cubs, some snowflakes and snow on the ground around the big bear's paws and the sleigh. Tear off the vellum below the bears. Score and fold a flap 1.5cm (⅝in) wide along the opposite side.

3 Hook the flap over the top of the folded card and secure to the card back with a glue stick. Tear a strip of white card and punch a white card circle. Arrange and glue in place on the card under the vellum. Punch a hole either side of the vellum panel at the bottom with a 4mm (⅛in) holepunch and set the eyelets to secure it to the card front (see page 101).

As an alternative to eyelets, tie a length of ribbon around the card to hold the vellum in place.

39 In Our Thoughts

Bring additional, subtle emphasis and dimension to an image stamped on vellum with embossing.

A small halo of embossed lines around this bunch of lilies is just enough to give it extra focus. The crisp white cross is simple and effective as a symbol of remembrance.

By adding ribbon and glitter, this design could be used for a wedding.

You will need ■ lilies rubber stamp ■ gamma green Brilliance™ inkpad ■ plain vellum ■ green mirror card ■ white textured folded card 15cm (6in) square ■ white textured card ■ 4 gold brads ■ die-cutting tool and cross die

1 Using the inkpad, stamp the lilies on vellum. Leave the ink to dry. Trim the vellum to 13 x 10cm (5 x 4in). Turn over and place on a foam mat. Use a fine ball embossing tool to add shading and highlights to the lilies with a mixture of lines and solid areas. Add a halo of crosshatching around the image.

2 Cut a piece of green mirror card 13.5 x 10.5cm (5¼ x 4¼in). Centre the vellum on the card and punch a hole in each corner with a 1.5mm (¹⁄₁₆in) holepunch. Insert brads to secure the vellum to the card.

3 Trim a strip 3cm (1⅛in) wide from the right-hand side of the folded card front. Stick a narrow strip of green mirror card down the right-hand side of the folded card back. Mount the lily panel on the card. Die-cut a cross from white textured card (see pages 40–43). Attach with adhesive foam pads.

40 Flower Jewel

Emboss marks and patterns to fill the open spaces of a design stamped on vellum.

Each section of this jewel motif has been layered to add depth and interest. Gems glued to the vellum lend an appropriate sparkle to this pretty greetings card.

Always test to see if the adhesive you plan to use is suitable for the particular type of vellum.

You will need ■ jewel-patterned rubber stamp ■ Victorian violet Brilliance™ inkpad ■ plain vellum ■ white textured folded card 14cm (5½in) square ■ pale plum, plum and dark plum card ■ paisley patterned vellum 13.5cm (5¼in) square ■ gems

1 Using the inkpad, stamp the image four times on plain vellum. Leave to dry. Separate the images if on one sheet. Each print will contribute one layer to the design, so only emboss one of the following on each: design outline, the eight large petals and four points, small square and tiny flower with points.

2 Cut out the embossed sections. Applying dots of Hi-Tack Glue™ with a cocktail stick to the edges of the vellum, layer the sections

one on top of the other. Mount on a piece of pale plum card 8cm (3¼in) square, then on plum card 9cm (3½in) square and finally onto a slightly larger piece of dark plum card.

3 Apply a tiny dot of Hi-Tack Glue™ to each corner of the patterned vellum and mount on the folded card. Mount the jewel panel on the card. Add gems using Hi-Tack Glue™.

Chalks & Perfect Pearls

Few experienced stampers would be without a box of chalks. They can be used for colouring in, dusting over torn card edges and applying over the wet surface of a stamped image on card. Perfect Pearls™ can be mixed with water to create a paint medium (see Shimmering Fall, page 23) and, like chalks, dusted over a wet image, in this case for a pearlescent effect.

You will need ■ candle and foliage rubber stamp ■ VersaMark™ inkpad ■ box of decorators' chalks ■ purple Sakura Moonlight™ pen ■ pale blue textured card ■ plum card 11.5 x 12.5cm (4½ x 5in) ■ purple card ■ white textured folded card 13.5cm (5¼in) square ■ two-tone blue/red sheer ribbon ■ holographic glitter glue

1 Ink up the stamp with the VersaMark™ pad. As the ink is clear, check carefully that the rubber is completely covered. Stamp the candle on the textured side of the pale blue card – the chalks will key more easily onto this surface.

2 Pick up some pale blue chalk by rubbing a small piece of cotton wool on the tablet in the tray. Dust very gently over the stamped surface and cover the whole image. This will seal the surface so that you do not have to worry about the ink drying out as you add other colours.

3 Build up the paler tones on the candle and foliage using pink, lilac and blue chalks. Apply patches of colour at random using the same dusting technique. Never rub the surface, as you could lift the ink. Always use a fresh piece of cotton wool for each new colour.

Chalks can be layered over a wet stamped image to build up a soft, tonal design.

This technique is ideal to use with solid and semi-solid stamps, which are sometimes harder to work with. Although chalks are delicate, they can pick up the detail in stamped images beautifully, as seen here in the candle and foliage. This striking, moody colour scheme lends an exotic richness to a traditional festive motif.

If you are concerned about the chalks rubbing off, spray the panel with artists' fixative or hair spray before mounting on the card.

(4)

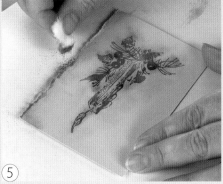

(5)

(6)

4 Add the darker tones using green and dark blue chalks to complete the dusting of the candle and foliage. Use some of the chalks dusted on the image to colour part of the background.

5 Trim the card down to a panel 11.5 x 10cm (4½ x 4in). Tear away a strip about 1cm (³⁄₈in) wide from the right-hand side of the panel. Use pieces of cotton wool to dust the torn edge with the chalk colours.

6 Highlight some of the detail on the candle and foliage with the purple pen – use small broken lines rather than drawing a complete outline. Punch two holes at the base of the candle with a 1.5mm (¹⁄₁₆in) holepunch. Thread the ribbon through and tie in a bow.

To Finish

⑦ *Mount the panel on the plum card, close to the left-hand edge, then tear down the right-hand side of the panel.*

⑨ *Highlight the candle, foliage and berries with the glitter glue. Add a ribbon bow.*

⑧ *Cut a wide strip from purple and pale blue textured card 11.5cm (4½in) long and tear down the right-hand side. Glue the purple strip behind the right-hand side of the torn plum card, then the pale blue strip behind the purple. Mount the layers on the folded card.*

42 Rose Gift Box

Construct an extra-special gift box from card stamped and dusted with chalks.

I chose yellow roses for this design, but you could easily change the colours to match the colour scheme of the occasion. The box is perfect for luxury chocolates.

You will need ■ roses rubber stamp ■ VersaMark™ inkpad ■ box of decorators' chalks ■ sheet of A4 (US letter) cream card ■ holographic glitter glue ■ sheer orange/gold ribbon

For a greater range of colours, try using artists' chalks. Simply rub the chalk onto scrap paper and pick up with a piece of cotton wool.

1 Use the template on page 116 to make your own template from scrap card. Draw around it onto the cream card with a pencil. Mark the position of the two holes. Cut out the box. Rub out any visible pencil lines.

2 Using the VersaMark™ inkpad, stamp two or three roses on the box. Dust with pale yellow chalk to seal. Repeat, working from one side of the box to the other, until covered. Dust orange, vermillion and dark red chalks over the roses. Highlight with the glitter glue and leave to dry. Punch the holes with a 4mm (⅛in) 'anywhere' holepunch.

3 Score along the fold lines with a medium ball embossing tool and fold up the box. Apply glue to one flap at a time and hold in place until bonded. Cut two lengths of ribbon and thread one through each hole. Tie a knot in the ends inside the box, close the box and tie the other ends in a bow.

43 Budding Artist

Use cotton wool to dust chalk over larger areas of a design and cotton buds to add finer detail.

For added fun, I have turned this stamped panel into a painting, set on a triangular folded card for an easel.

You will need ■ hedgehog artist and snail model rubber stamp ■ graphite black Brilliance™ inkpad ■ box of decorators' chalks ■ white card ■ lilac, pale lilac, brown, grey and pink textured card ■ 2 lime green brads ■ die-cutting tool and snail die-cut

1 Using the inkpad, stamp the image onto white card. Leave to dry. Colour in with chalks using cotton wool for the open spaces (e.g. sky) and cotton buds for the small areas (e.g. snail). Trim to 7 x 10.5cm (2¾ x 4¼in).

2 Mount onto slightly larger pieces of lilac, then pale lilac card. Cut a card triangle with a 13cm (5in) base and 14cm (5½in) sides. Use to cut two adjoining triangles from brown card. Score and fold along the adjoining line.

3 Draw two inner lines parallel to and 2.5cm (1in) from the triangle sides. Cut along the lines through both card thicknesses. Mount the hedgehog panel on the top section of the card. Punch two holes at the base of the panel with a 4mm (⅛in) holepunch and insert the brads. Die-cut a snail from grey and pink card (see pages 40–43). Mount on the easel with adhesive foam pads.

For an even softer look and outline, stamp the image in brown ink.

44 Peacock Feather

Achieve impactful iridescent effects by using Perfect Pearls™ on dark card.

If you remove too much powder or want to blend other colours in after Step 1, you can still do so.

This technique is used here to capture the fabulous shimmering colours of a peacock feather. Using pearlescent card for the mounting and layering enhances the colours.

You will need ■ rubber stamps – peacock feather; paisley-type pattern ■ VersaMark™ inkpad ■ Perfect Pearls™ – sunflower sparkle, kiwi, blue smoke, turquoise ■ black card ■ gold foiled paper ■ pearlescent teal folded card 14 x 11cm (5½ x 4½in) ■ pearlescent teal card 11.5 x 5.5cm (4½ x 2¼in) ■ 2 gold eyelets ■ dusting brush

1 Using the VersaMark™ inkpad, stamp the feather onto black card. Gently dab a little Perfect Pearls™ over the wet image. Repeat with the next colour and so on until coloured in. Brush off the excess powder with the dusting brush. Trim to 11 x 5cm (4¼ x 2in).

2 Using the VersaMark™ inkpad, stamp the paisley pattern onto black card. Dust with Perfect Pearls™. Trim to 13 x 9.5cm (5 x 3¾in).

Mount onto a slightly larger piece of the gold paper. Mount on the folded card.

3 Glue a strip of torn gold paper about 3.5cm (1⅜in) wide across the card front. Punch two holes in the right-hand end with a 4mm (⅛in) holepunch and set the eyelets (see page 101). Cover the bottom half of the teal card with gold paper. Mount the feather panel, then mount on the folded card.

Bleaching

Bleach can be used as a painting medium to produce different shades of one colour within a stamped image for a monochromatic effect or to remove the colour from dark card to create a lighter base to work on. You can also apply thick bleach direct to the rubber and stamp with it instead of ink. Not all card can be bleached, so always test to see how well the technique works.

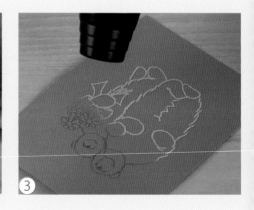

You will need ■ bear couple with posy rubber stamp ■ VersaMark™ inkpad ■ clear embossing powder ■ thick bleach ■ Sakura Gelly Roll Glaze™ pens – red, yellow ■ white Sakura Soufflé™ pen ■ brown card 12.5 x 10cm (5 x 4in) ■ tan card 13.5 x 12cm (5¼ x 4¾in) ■ cream hammer-textured folded card 14.5cm (5¾in) square ■ pale yellow and white textured card ■ die-cutting tool and large oval die ■ 4 gold brads ■ small flower punch ■ anti-static puff

1

2

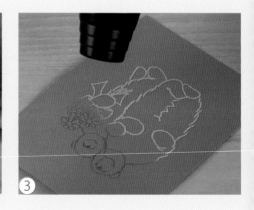

3

1 Rub the anti-static puff all over the brown card – over time, card absorbs moisture from the air, and this, combined with static, can make removing embossing powder specks difficult.

2 Using the VersaMark™ inkpad, stamp the image on the tan card. Sprinkle a thin layer of clear embossing powder all over the image. Tip off the excess, then return it to the jar.

3 Heat the surface of the embossing powder with a heat gun (see page 29). Make sure that all the powder has melted and that the outline of the bears has risen. Don't overheat the powder, as the lines will sink and appear oily.

Use bleach to remove varying degrees of colour from dark-coloured card to create a textural effect.

Here, this bleaching technique has been used to create the impression of fur on the stamped bears. In order to control the shading and to achieve a variety of tones, allow each application of bleach a few minutes to work to gauge the full effect before applying further layers of bleach. As these two cuddly bears make such a happy, romantic couple, this card would be perfect for celebrating a wedding anniversary in memorable style.

As bleach reacts to light, you can leave it on a sunny windowsill to increase the bleaching effect.

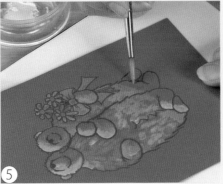

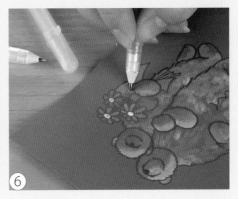

4 Protect your work surface with scrap paper. Pour a small quantity of bleach into a jar. Using a fine paintbrush and clean water, dilute a little of the bleach and paint onto the bears in small strokes, leaving some areas untouched. Paint the bouquet entirely with bleach.

5 Leave to dry. You can speed up the drying with the heat gun, but avoid overheating the embossing. Apply more bleach if you need to lighten some areas further. Paint strokes of bleach around the bears' feet to create ground. Colour in the bouquet with the glaze pens. Leave to dry.

6 Die-cut an oval aperture in the tan card (see pages 40–43). Glue to the bear panel to frame the bears. Mount on the folded card. Punch holes in the frame corners with a 1.5mm (1/16in) holepunch and insert brads. Punch small yellow flowers and white centres. Assemble and mount at random.

46 Lavender Landscape

47 One Frosty Night

Use bleaching to create an atmospheric three-dimensional landscape.

I have bleached out the card in the background here, added clouds and created depth by making the mountains and foreground lighter. The flowers mimic a hedge that you look over to admire the lavender.

You will need ■ lavender field rubber stamp ■ VersaMark™ inkpad ■ clear embossing powder ■ thick bleach ■ colouring pencils ■ lavender card 8 x 10.5cm (3¼ x 4¼in) ■ pale lavender, lilac and white textured card ■ white hammer-textured folded card 14.5 x 12cm (5¾ x 4¾in), fold at the top ■ mini flower corner punch ■ die-cutting tool and large scallop-edged frame die

Make a stamped image stand out against the background by bleaching out a frame.

In this case, the dark indigo blue card has bleached to purple to frame the reindeer. Metallic pencils add a festive frosting to the design.

You will need ■ reindeer rubber stamp ■ VersaMark™ inkpad ■ clear embossing powder ■ thick bleach ■ clear Sakura Gelly Roll Glaze™ pen ■ silver colouring pencil ■ indigo blue card 13 x 10cm (5 x 4in) ■ silver foiled paper ■ plum textured card 15 x 11cm (6 x 4¼in) ■ silver linen-effect folded card 15.5 x 11.5cm (6¼ x 4½in) ■ medium snowflake punch ■ silver cord

It is easier to layer and punch two or more snowflakes at a time as the foil is so delicate.

1 Using the inkpad and embossing powder, stamp and heat emboss the landscape onto the lavender card (see pages 28–31).

Be careful not to chip the embossed lines by pushing against them with the tips of the pencils as you colour.

2 Using a fine paintbrush and clean water, dilute a little of the bleach and paint over parts of the field, tree, house, mountains and sky. Use the bleach to extend the field beyond the embossed frame. Using colouring pencils, apply some colour detail to the embossed landscape.

3 Punch out several tiny flowers from the pale lavender, lilac and white card. Glue around the embossed frame. Die-cut a large scallop-edged frame from the pale lavender card (see pages 40–43). Glue over the landscape and mount on the folded card.

1 Using the inkpad and embossing powder, stamp and emboss the image onto the indigo blue card (see pages 28–31). Tear down to 10.5 x 8.5cm (4¼ x 3½in). Using a fine paintbrush and water, dilute a little bleach and paint over the reindeer's body and in patches over the background. Leave to dry.

2 Draw over the open spaces of the reindeer's body with the glaze pen. Shade the gaps between the bleached

patches on the background with silver pencil. Mount the panel on the silver paper and tear the sides, leaving a narrow border. Glue some of the leftover torn paper onto the panel to create ground.

3 Mount the plum card on the folded card. Glue the reindeer panel in place. Punch two snowflakes from the silver paper and add to the panel. Wrap a double length of silver cord around the card front and tie in a knot.

48 Irises

Apply thick bleach directly to a stamp's rubber to produce a tonal image on dark card.

You can use any type of stamp, but generally the technique works best with solid images. Subtle colour has been added to these irises with colouring pencils.

You will need ■ irises rubber stamp ■ thick bleach ■ colouring pencils ■ galaxy gold Brilliance™ inkpad ■ burgundy card 9 x 12.5cm (3½ x 5in) ■ cream pearlescent folded card 18 x 11.5cm (7 x 4½in), fold at the top ■ 4 burgundy eyelets

When using bleach for stamping, always remember to clean the stamp straight away so that it doesn't damage the rubber.

1 Use a sponge dauber to dab bleach onto the stamp rubber, applying a generous layer. Stamp onto the burgundy card. Put extra pressure on the stamp to make sure that the bleach soaks right into the card. Leave to dry naturally or use a heat gun to speed up the process.

2 Use a fine paintbrush and clean water to dilute a little of the bleach, then apply over any areas of the image that need to be sharper and to bleach out more colour from the card. Refer to the image on the decal as a guide.

3 Place the panel on a foam mat and use a fine ball embossing tool to draw a broken outline around the image. Using colouring pencils, apply colour detail to the flowers, leaves and stems. Using the inkpad, stamp a row of irises along the front of the folded card.

4 Cover most of the irises on the burgundy card with a piece of torn paper. Sponge ink over the torn edge onto the card. Remove the paper. Add gold touches to the sky. Mount on the folded card. Punch holes in the corners with a 4mm (⅛in) holepunch. Set the eyelets (see page 101).

Collage

Creating a collage involves selecting and arranging a variety of different elements in a grouping that is pleasing to the eye. You can include any item you like, from a picture to a three-dimensional object, but it is invariably easier to compose a collage around a particular theme. Stamping images for a collage gives you greater creative scope, as they can be specifically tailored to your chosen theme. The same stamp can be used again and again, coloured in, positioned and cut out in endless different ways.

You will need ■ plain papier mâché box with hinged lid ■ sun, Saturn and shooting star stained glass-style set of rubber stamps ■ acrylic paint – pale blue, ultramarine blue ■ Black StazOn™ inkpad ■ colouring pencils ■ thin white paper ■ star gems ■ découpage glue

1 Using a medium-sized paintbrush, apply a coat of pale blue paint all over the inside and outside of the box. Thin the paint with a little water if it is difficult to spread. It is best to apply two thin coats rather than one thick coat, leaving the paint to dry between coats.

2 Using a small sponge, apply a thin coat of ultramarine blue paint all over the inside and outside of the box, allowing the pale blue coat to show through. You only need to use a very small amount of paint and it can be dragged and dabbed on for a distressed look.

3 Using the black inkpad, stamp at least four images from each of the three stamps onto white paper. Use paper that is thin enough to mould itself to the curved surface of the box lid when the découpage glue is applied – standard photocopying paper is ideal.

49 Celestial Box

Design and create your own découpage papers by selecting stamp designs of the same style, printing them onto thin white paper and colouring in to coordinate with the scheme.

The celestial theme is perfect for transforming this plain box into a sumptuous jewellery casket, and the star gems add a complementary finishing touch. The stained-glass style of the stamps lends the images to being cut out, as the outlines are bold and simple.

When working with découpage glue, always use mediums that are waterproof/permanent, such as the StazOn™ inkpad and the colouring pencils used in this project.

(4)

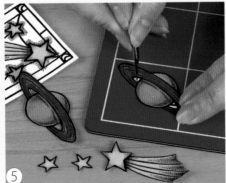
(5)

(6)

4 Using colouring pencils, colour in the whole sun images, the Saturns and the shooting stars only without their surrounding designs, together with some of the small stars from the images. Use pencils that have soft leads for good coverage.

5 Cut out the images you have coloured in with a small pair of scissors, cutting slightly into the black outline to avoid leaving any white paper behind. Working on a cutting mat, use a craft knife to remove the white areas around the planets.

6 Work out where to place each image. Using a paintbrush, apply a thin coat of découpage glue over the first area. Position the image and use the brush to paste it down, adding extra glue. Continue in the same way. Coat the entire box with glue. Add the gems with Hi-Tack Glue™.

Collages with a vintage look can be created by combining retro stamp designs in a muted colour scheme and using antiquing effects.

This collaged pocket holding a matching tag has been worked predominantly in soft browns, but to give these a lift, touches of green, glue and white have been added, echoing the colours of the torn patterned paper and postage stamp. As a birthday bonus, the tag can double up as a bookmark.

You will need ■ rubber stamps – vintage car; clock, postmark and script ■ Brilliance™ inkpads – coffee bean, graphite black ■ colouring pencils – ochre, lime green, white, yellow, dark brown ■ sand card ■ cream linen-effect folded card 18 x 9cm (7 x 3½in) ■ green paper ■ parcel paper 19 x 7cm (7½ x 2¾in) ■ cream linen-effect card ■ tag punch ■ die-cutting tool and plane and Eiffel Tower dies ■ copper eyelets ■ dark brown button ■ string ■ postage stamp

> If an item you want to include in a collage looks too new to use, such as a postage stamp, apply some brown ink with a sponge to age the item.

1 Using the brown inkpad, stamp the car once and the other designs twice on the sand card. Use the colouring pencils to add colour highlights, allowing some of the base card to show through. Use a dark brown pencil to add detail over the stamped lines. Tear out the car.

2 On the front panel of the folded card, cut 11cm (4½in) from the bottom edge on the left-hand side to 2.5cm (1in) on the right-hand side. Cover the back panel and front flap with the stamped card, adding pieces of the torn green paper. Round off the top corners with a corner rounder.

3 Scrunch up the parcel paper. Flatten out and glue to a slightly larger piece of the cream card. Cut a panel 15.5 x 6.5cm (6¼ x 2½in) and punch a tag from the covered card. Round off the corners. Die-cut a plane and Eiffel Tower. Sponge both tags and die-cuts with the inks.

4 Secure the front flap to the back panel with the eyelets (see page 101). Add the Eiffel Tower and button. Mount the plane on the small tag. Punch the tag holes and fix the eyelet. Thread with string. Add the stamp and car to the large tag. Mount the small tag with adhesive foam pads.

51 Garden Windows

Combine stamped images and die-cuts that contrast in style in a collage unified by the colour scheme.

Use this dreamy garden to send your best wishes to someone special.

When you are picking up ink directly from an inkpad with a wet paintbrush for painting, always use the side of the pad.

You will need ■ rubber stamps – sketched daisy; set of garden flower and bugs stamps, some framed ■ Brilliance™ inkpads – aurora and graphite black ■ white linen-effect card 16.5cm (6½in) square ■ white, pastel yellow, peach card ■ pink narrow ribbon ■ die-cutting tool and large flower head dies ■ pastel eyelets – round, flower

1 Using the aurora inkpad, stamp the sketched daisy all over the linen-effect card. Using a wet paintbrush, apply thin washes of the aurora inks to highlight, then sponge yellow ink in between the highlights. Score 5.5cm (2¼in) from one side on the reverse. Turn the card over and score 11cm (4½in) from the same side. Carefully fold so that the score lines are inside the folds. Trim the top corners of each panel. Punch holes with a 6mm (¼in) holepunch. Thread each of the holes with ribbon.

2 Using the black inkpad, stamp unframed flowers, butterflies and a ladybird onto the tags. Stamp several framed motifs onto white card. Colour in using the three aurora inks. Cut out the framed motifs with small scissors.

3 Die-cut flower heads from yellow and peach card. Arrange with the framed motifs on the tags and attach some boxes with adhesive foam pads. Punch holes through the die-cut flowers and set with eyelets (see page 101).

52 Three Today

Select a single stamp made up of different simple components and rearrange the individual elements to create a bold collage.

The stripy paper inspired the colour scheme for the card, but it could easily be changed to something softer and more decorative to celebrate a girl's birthday.

Use the spare stamped elements, such as the second lion and giraffe, for decorating an envelope for the card.

You will need ■ animals rubber stamp ■ Mediterranean blue Brilliance™ inkpad ■ felt-tip pens – blue, green ■ white, pastel green and blue card ■ blue folded card 14cm (5½in) square ■ blue and green striped paper ■ die-cutting tool and number 3 die ■ 4 pastel blue brads ■ blue narrow sheer ribbon ■ green and white spotted button

1 Using the blue inkpad, stamp the animals stamp twice onto white card and cut out two elephants, two fish, one lion and one giraffe. Run each felt-tip pen over a plastic lid. Use a wet paintbrush to pick up the ink and apply washes to colour in the animals.

2 Cover part of the blue folded card with the striped paper, leaving a blue border 4.5cm (1¾in) wide on the left-hand side. Die-cut the number three from pastel green card (see pages 40–43). Mount on a piece of blue card 4.5 x 3.5cm (1¾ x 1⅜in). Punch a hole in each corner with a 1.5mm (¹⁄₁₆in) holepunch and insert a brad.

3 Thread a short length of the ribbon through the holes of the button and tie in a double knot. Arrange and mount the animal and number panels and button onto the folded card, raising some of the panels with adhesive foam pads.

Découpage

This paper crafting technique involves cutting out printed images and gluing them to a flat surface, and is useful for adding extra interest to your stamped images. Great results can be achieved by being selective and cutting out only part of an image or layering up cutout sections to create a three-dimensional image. Be sure to use a small, sharp pair of scissors for accurate cutting.

You will need ■ large and tiny Easter bunny, basket, egg border and small flower set of clear stamps ■ clear acrylic block ■ graphite black Brilliance™ inkpad ■ brush markers ■ fine line black pen ■ smooth white card ■ yellow and green printed papers ■ white textured folded card 16 x 11cm (6¼ x 4½in) ■ die-cutting tool and large tag die ■ green brad

1 Using the inkpad, stamp three large bunnies, one basket, one egg border and one tiny bunny onto smooth white card. As the stamps are clear, you can stamp the images individually or place all the dies on the acrylic block and stamp in one go.

2 Run the brush markers over a plastic lid. Dip a fine paintbrush into clean water, pick up some of the ink and colour in the images. To add depth, paint a pale blue line around the body parts of the large bunnies and the tiny bunny's head.

3 Use a small, sharp pair of scissors to cut out the images, cutting very slightly into the outline so that none of the white card remains, as this may show up if mounted on a coloured background. Use a craft knife on a cutting mat to cut away the inside section of the basket.

Create an impressive three-dimensional découpage design by printing and layering selected motifs from a set of clear stamps (see pages 36–39).

The task of cutting out the bunny for this design is made simple by the fact that the different body parts are easy to distinguish. Individual eggs are also easily cut from the border stamp. By colouring in all the stamped images for this Easter card at the same time, you avoid mismatched tones.

Write or stamp a surprise message on the card, which is revealed only when the tag is swung to one side.

4 Keeping one large bunny intact, remove the back leg and paw from another bunny and all but the head and arm from the remaining one. Cut out the eggs you need from the egg border.

5 Place adhesive foam pads on the back of the sections for layering, spacing them out so that there is support all round the edges and in the centre. Add the layers to the whole bunny – always build up an image with the biggest section at the bottom to the smallest at the top.

6 Die-cut a large tag from the yellow paper (see pages 40–43). Place the small flower die on the acrylic block. Using the inkpad, stamp the flower at random all over the tag, working from the top to the bottom.

(7)

7 Use the fine tips of the brush markers to colour in the flowers. Die-cut a tag from the green paper, tear off the bottom and glue to the yellow tag. Draw small dotted lines with the black pen on the green paper.

(8)

8 Cut a 2cm (¾in) wide green paper strip. Fold in half at an angle and glue over the tag hole. Mount the bunny. Attach the two eggs to the basket back. Apply glue to the basket back and slide it between the bunny's paws and over the back foot. Use tweezers to tuck the single egg in between its paws. Mount the tiny bunny with adhesive foam pads.

(9)

9 Glue a 10cm (4in) wide band of the yellow paper to the folded card front. Stamp flowers along the base. Colour in with brush markers, adding black pen dots in between. Punch a hole in the folded strip at the tag top and near the card top with a 4mm (⅙in) holepunch. Place the tag on the card, aligning the holes. Insert the brad.

54 A Gift of Love

Choose a stamped image with lots of detail and build up several layers of découpage.

Three prints of the mice were used to create this playful design, perfect for a child's birthday.

You will need ■ mice and letter rubber stamp ■ coffee bean Brilliance™ inkpad ■ colouring pencils ■ cream, red and tan card ■ ochre folded card 15 x 11cm (6 x 4½in)

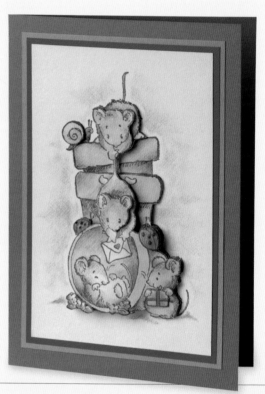

1 Stamp the image three times on cream card. Keep one image as a base for layering. Trim the card to 12.5 x 8.5cm (5 x 3½in). Colour the images with colouring pencils. Only colour in the sections on the base that will be visible after layering and the background. Colour the sections on the others that will be cut out.

2 Use small, sharp scissors to cut out the images. Curl the pieces around a round pencil, rocking it back and forth in the palm of your hand. Slice off a blob of silicone glue

from the tube with a cocktail stick. Place several blobs on the back of the largest cutout and press down gently on the base. Continue to build layers.

3 Cut a piece of red card 13 x 9cm (5¼ x 3¾in). Mount the mice panel on this, then layer onto a slightly larger piece of tan card. Mount the panel centrally on the folded card.

Colour around the edges of the sections that will be layered – they may be visible from the side.

55 Two of a Kind

Stamp an image directly onto printed paper for layering, using the colour and pattern of the paper to fill in the image.

These giraffes have been printed on animal-print paper, then cut out and layered over a second print.

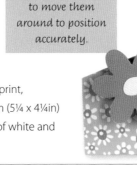

Use a glue stick for gluing the cutouts to the print, as it allows you time to move them around to position accurately.

You will need ■ mother and baby giraffes rubber stamp ■ graphite black Brilliance™ inkpad ■ fine line black pen ■ animal-print, spotted and floral printed papers ■ pink textured card 13.5 x 10.5cm (5¼ x 4¼in) ■ 2 pieces of green textured card 8.5 x 12cm (3½ x 4¾in) ■ scraps of white and pink card ■ 6 white eyelets ■ die-cutting tool and daisy dies

1 Stamp the giraffes on animal-print paper. Cut out, snipping off the tails, horns and manes. Cut two panels of contrasting printed papers 13 x 10cm (5 x 4in). Cut a rounded section from the bottom of one. Draw a black stitched line along the curve. Glue to the other. Stamp on the giraffes. Glue the cutouts onto the print. Mount on the pink card.

2 Cover the green card pieces with printed paper. Paper side facing, cut one from the left-hand corner to a point 4cm (1½in) up on the right-hand side. Repeat with the other piece, green side facing. Score and fold a narrow flap down the uncut end of each, folding the rest of each panel in half.

3 Glue the flaps to the main panel back. Punch three holes down each side of the main panel with a 4mm (⅛in) holepunch and set the eyelets to secure the flaps further (see page 101). Die-cut and assemble several flowers from white and pink card (see pages 40–43). Mount on the card with adhesive foam pads.

56 Mr and Mrs Frosty

Stamp an image on several printed paper backgrounds so that you can use different sections for découpage.

As the sections for layering are quite small, choose papers with small patterns and those that are thin, so that the layering is almost invisible.

Using printed papers from a single collection will make it easier to colour coordinate the design.

You will need ■ snow couple rubber stamp ■ graphite black Brilliance™ inkpad ■ orange brush marker ■ blue and lilac printed papers ■ white linen-effect card ■ lilac textured card 9 x 13cm (3½ x 5in) ■ white linen-effect folded card 16 x 11.5cm (6¼ x 4½in), fold at the top ■ 4 aqua blue brads ■ lilac gingham ribbon ■ holographic glitter glue

1 Using the inkpad, stamp the image three times on different printed papers and once on white card (the latter will be the base image). Trim the card to 8 x 12cm (3¼ x 4¾in). Cut out sections of the paper-stamped images to layer on the base, such as the scarves and hearts.

2 Colour in the noses with the orange brush marker. Cut a piece of printed paper 8 x 12cm (3¼ x 4¾in) and tear off the corners. Glue to the corners of the white panel. Mount the panel on the lilac card. Punch a hole in each corner of the white panel with a 1.5mm (¹⁄₁₆in) holepunch and insert a brad.

3 Stick lengths of ribbon in a cross formation on the folded card with Hi-Tack Glue™. Mount the panel on the card with adhesive foam pads. Highlight the snow couple with the glitter glue.

Shaped Cards

Most people tend to use square and rectangular-shaped cards for stamped designs, as they are easy to work with, but there are lots of different shaped cards on the market that offer much creative potential. If you really like a challenge, why not try designing your own card shapes? It's not as difficult as you might think! Experiment with some scrap card to see what you can come up with.

You will need ■ lion rubber stamp ■ black graphite Brilliance™ inkpad ■ black Sakura Gelly Roll Glaze™ pen ■ orange folded card 16 x 14cm (6¼ x 5½in), fold at the top ■ lime green, yellow, orange and fuchsia card ■ 2.5cm (1in) circle punch ■ die-cutting tool and number dies ■ sheer ribbon for the optional tag

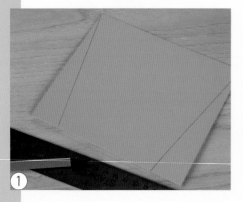

(1)

(2)

(3)

1 Mark two points along the fold of the folded card 3cm (1⅛in) in from each side. Use a pencil and metal ruler to draw two lines linking the points to the corners of the card at the base.

2 Place the card on a cutting mat. Lay the ruler next to the pencil line and use a craft knife to cut through both thicknesses of card. Make sure that the blade is sharp – a blunt blade could snag the card as you cut through.

3 Using the inkpad, stamp the lion at random all over the card front, starting from one side. Re-ink the rubber between each print and alter the angle of each print to add interest to the pattern. Also stamp a single lion on lime green, yellow and orange card. Leave to dry.

Try cutting away the sides of a standard square folded card to transform almost instantly the basic shape.

In this case, a square card is turned into a gift box shape, which has been stamped with a motif all over at random to mimic wrapping paper. For this child's birthday design I chose an endearingly playful little lion rubber stamp and used a range of bright colours that would have immediate appeal to young ones.

Use the lion stamp to create coordinating invitations for a birthday party.

④

⑤

⑥

4 Using the glaze pen, colour in the noses of the lions on the folded card and the nose of the lion on the orange card. Leave the glaze to dry for a few minutes before handling the card and panel.

5 Cut out the lion from the yellow card, leaving a narrow border. From the green card you only need to cut out the head and mane, and from the orange card just the head. Attach adhesive foam pads to the back of each piece and layer up ready to add to the card.

6 Using the circle punch, punch a semicircle from yellow card, working with the punch upside down to aid positioning. Cut two strips of green card 1.5 x 16cm (⅝ x 6¼in) for the ribbon and a strip of yellow and pink card 5mm (³⁄₁₆in) wide for making the confetti.

7 Die-cut a number appropriate for the birthday from pink card (see pages 40–43). Use the bow template on page 116 to make your own template from scrap card. Draw around the bow section twice onto green card with a pencil and cut out.

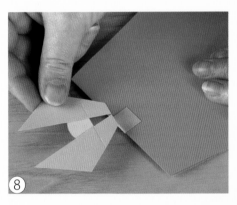

8 Glue the green strips in a cross on the card front, folding over the excess at the top and trimming the other ends. Glue the bow sections to the semicircle. Score a line below the semicircle to allow the bow to stand upright when the card is standing. Glue the bow to the card top – the semicircle should butt against the spine.

9 Cut the narrow pink and yellow strips into small pieces of confetti. Glue at random all over the card. Mount the lion and number onto the centre of the card with adhesive foam pads. Make a matching tag.

58 Gone Shopping

Create a card that looks like a shopping bag using stamps, dies and punches.

The curved handles were made by cutting an oval die-cut in half and punching out the centre with a circle punch.

You will need ■ small flower rubber stamp ■ VersaColor™ inkpads – brown, cyan blue ■ smooth white card 18 x 22cm (7 x 8¾in) ■ blue and brown card ■ punches – 1cm (⅜in), 4cm (1½in) and 2.5cm (1in) circle, large flower ■ brown eyelets ■ die-cutting tool and large oval die

> Instead of die-cut handles, cut two card rectangles in half, round off the corners with a punch and cut away the inner sections.

1 Use the template on page 117 to make your own template from scrap card. Draw around it onto the white card with a pencil. Cut out with a craft knife and ruler on a cutting mat.

2 Using the brown and blue inkpads separately, stamp the flower at random all over the card. Sponge the card edges with blue ink. Using the 1cm (⅜in) circle punch, punch flower centres from blue and brown card. Glue to the flowers. Glue a blue card strip across both bag sides and set the eyelets (see page 101).

3 Die-cut an oval from blue card (see pages 40–43), cut in half and remove the centres with the 4cm (1½in) circle punch. Glue in place and set the eyelets. Score along the score lines and fold up the bag. Punch two brown flowers and 2.5cm (1cm) blue circles. Punch a 1cm (⅜in) hole in both circles. Assemble the flowers and set an eyelet in each flower centre. Mount with adhesive foam pads. Round off the corners of a small brown rectangle with a corner rounder punch. Fold in half and glue to the bag top as a clasp.

59 The Witch's Hat

Use a strip of card to transform a simple triangular-shaped card into a hat.

In this case, the hat is themed for Halloween, stamped with a bat motif and embossed with a holographic powder for a sparkly effect.

Turn the hat into a wizard's hat for a Harry Potter fan.

You will need ■ bat, cat, haunted house, pumpkin set of rubber stamps ■ VersaMark™ inkpad ■ black graphite Brilliance™ inkpad ■ holographic embossing powder ■ black, green, purple and orange card ■ die-cutting tool and frame die ■ ribbon – orange gingham, sheer black ■ tag punch ■ 3 black eyelets

1 Cut a card triangle with a 15cm (6in) base and 20cm (8in) sides. Use to cut two adjoining black card triangles. Score and fold in between. Using the VersaMark™ inkpad, stamp and heat emboss with bats (see pages 28–31). Add a green card base. Mount a 2.5 x 17cm (1 x 6¾in) black card strip on the base.

2 Die-cut a frame from purple card and mount on the card with adhesive foam pads. Tie orange gingham ribbon to the frame. Using the black inkpad, stamp a cat, house and four pumpkins onto orange card. Punch out a cat and house tag. Cut out the pumpkins.

3 Add black ribbon to the tags. Carefully heat with a heat gun to curl. Punch three holes in the band with a 4mm (⅛in) holepunch and set eyelets (see page 101). Tie with ribbon. Heat to curl. Mount the tags and pumpkins.

60 What a Cracker!

Turn a long rectangular folded card into a cracker of a design!

For a festive frolic, I have decorated the central panel of this Christmas cracker with a cheeky silhouette stamp of Father Christmas kissing a girl under the mistletoe.

You will need ■ Father Christmas and girl under the mistletoe silhouette rubber stamp ■ black graphite Brilliance™ inkpad ■ white Sakura Soufflé™ Pen ■ white textured folded card 6.5 x 21cm (2½ x 8¼in) ■ gold linen-effect card ■ red and green card ■ holographic glitter glue ■ tiny star punch

Make some smaller crackers to use as place cards on the Christmas table.

1 Use the template on page 117 to make your own template from scrap card. Place the template on the folded card. You should only need to pencil in the 'V' shapes. However, if your card is larger than the template, line up the top of the cracker with the spine of the card and draw out the shape. Use scissors to cut out the necessary parts.

2 Cut two thin strips of gold, red and green card. Glue in a band across each end of the cracker. Make a larger band for the central panel with a wide strip of gold and a narrow strip of red card either side. Add the glitter glue to the ends of the cracker.

3 Using the inkpad, stamp the silhouette image onto red card. Highlight the image with the white pen. Trim the card to 5.5cm (2¼in) square. Mount on a slightly larger piece of green card. Mount the panel on the cracker with adhesive foam pads. Decorate with the glitter glue and tiny stars punched from the gold card.

Metal & Fun Foam

If you choose the appropriate inkpad, you can stamp onto a variety of different surfaces including metal and fun foam. A permanent inkpad is a must for metal, otherwise you need to emboss the image. If the metal is soft enough, you can draw into it with an embossing tool. You can stamp directly onto fun foam or press a stamp into the heated surface to create a relief print.

You will need ■ three Christmas trees rubber stamp ■ jet black StazOn™ inkpad ■ Sakura Gelly Roll Glaze™ pens – yellow, pink, purple ■ green overhead projector pen ■ gold lightweight metal foil ■ thick green vellum, torn to 7.5 x 10.5cm (3 x 4¼in) ■ fuchsia folded card 15 x 10.5cm (6 x 4¼in), fold at the top ■ 4 metallic purple brads

①

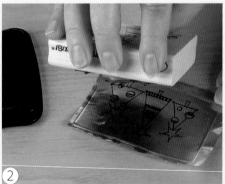

②

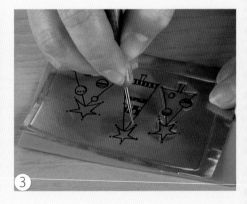

③

1 Using scissors, trim the foil slightly larger than the wood mount of the stamp. Place the stamp rubber side up on the foil. Use an embossing tool to draw around the wood mount. This will make it easier to trim the foil at a later stage.

2 Using the black inkpad, stamp the trees onto the foil within the frame. The surface is slippery, so press down slowly but firmly. The ink will only need a few minutes to dry, but you can speed up the process with a heat gun.

3 Place the foil on foam mat. Using a fine ball embossing tool, draw around the trees, trunks, stars, baubles and stripes into the surface of the foil – draw on the outside of the stamped line, so that you leave the stamped image intact.

Use permanent ink to stamp an image onto lightweight metal foil and enhance it by impressing the details into the metal.

Gold foil makes the ideal choice for this festive Christmas tree design, which is stamped with black permanent ink and coloured in with permanent pens. As the metal is quite thin, you can add extra detail by drawing into the metal.

You can use an empty ballpoint pen instead of an embossing tool to draw into the foil.

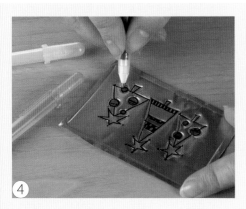

4 Colour in the detail on the trees with the glaze pens, using the yellow pen for the stars and the pink and purple pens for the baubles and the horizontal stripe on the central tree. Leave the glaze to dry thoroughly. If you need to touch up any area, allow the first layer to dry.

5 Use the overhead projector pen to colour in the green areas on the trees. Avoid touching the stamped outline with the pen, as it can lift the ink. Also, try to avoid working over the same area too much, as the colour can become muddy as a result.

6 Use a craft knife and metal ruler on a cutting mat to trim the foil. Mount the vellum on the folded card with double-sided adhesive tape placed away from the edges. Mount the foil panel with Hi-Tack Glue™. Punch holes in the corners with a 1.5mm (1/16in) holepunch. Insert the brads.

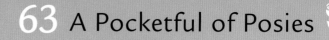

62 Jade Trinket Box

Create a stamped and indented decorative foil panel for a trinket box.

This plain wooden box has been sponged with jade pearlescent ink to complement the green foil, with the tops of metallic brads used to mimic metal studs.

You will need ■ plain wooden box with lid ■ landscape with sun rubber stamp ■ jet black StazOn™ inkpad ■ overhead projector pens – yellow, orange, pink, green ■ jade satin Mica Magic™ re-fill ink ■ green lightweight metal foil ■ 4 metallic green brads ■ wire cutters

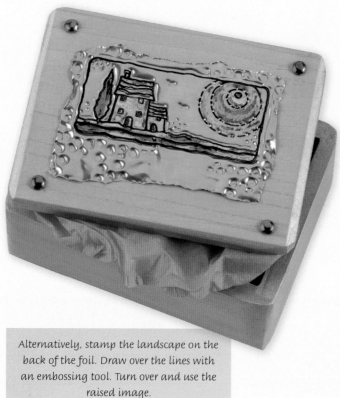

Alternatively, stamp the landscape on the back of the foil. Draw over the lines with an embossing tool. Turn over and use the raised image.

1 Using the black inkpad, stamp the landscape onto the foil. Leave to dry. Place the foil on a foam mat and draw around the trees, fields, house and sun with a fine ball embossing tool.

2 Highlight the trees, fields, house and sun with the overhead projector pens. Tear around the sides of the landscape frame, leaving an uneven border. Use the embossing tool to draw groups of dots into the surface of the foil around the landscape frame.

3 Use a sponge dauber to cover the box with the jade ink inside and out. Mount the foil panel on the box lid with Hi-Tack Glue™. Remove the 'wings' of the brads with wire cutters. Stick a brad head to each corner of the lid with Hi-Tack Glue™.

63 A Pocketful of Posies

Mimic the effect of fabric by stamping into hot fun foam and sponging with ink.

This technique creates a convincing denim effect, with the sponging highlighting the stamped stitching.

You will need ■ denim pocket rubber stamp ■ Mediterranean blue Brilliance™ inkpad ■ light blue fun foam ■ white textured folded card 14.5 x 10cm (5¾ x 4in) ■ blue plaid printed paper ■ pale yellow, yellow, marigold and orange textured card ■ 2 flower eyelets ■ punches – large, medium and small flower, ribbon ■ yellow gingham ribbon

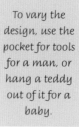

To vary the design, use the pocket for tools for a man, or hang a teddy out of it for a baby.

1 Using scissors, trim the fun foam slightly larger than the wood mount of the stamp. Heat the surface with a heat gun. Press the stamp firmly down into the hot foam. Hold for a few seconds, then lift the stamp off. Use a sponge dauber to apply blue ink lightly across the surface.

2 Cut out the pocket, leaving a very narrow border around the recessed outline. Punch two holes with a 4mm (⅛in) holepunch and set the eyelets (see page 101). Cover three-quarters of the folded card with the printed paper, adding a strip of pale yellow card down the right-hand edge. Trim the corners to make a tag.

3 Punch and assemble flowers from yellow and orange card. Use a 6mm (¼in) holepunch for the flower centres. Mount the pocket on the folded card with Hi-Tack Glue™. Make two slits in the card top with the ribbon punch. Thread through ribbon and tie in a knot. Arrange and mount the flowers on the card, raising a few with adhesive foam pads.

Try heating the surface of fun foam to stamp an image in relief.

The result is highly tactile, so great to use for a child's card or for someone who is visually impaired. To reflect the patchwork style of the elephant, I have created a background of punched squares and faux stitching. If you are not happy with your first print into the hot foam, you can reheat the foam to return it to its original flat state.

You will need ■ patchwork-style elephant rubber stamp ■ Victorian violet Brilliance™ inkpad ■ lilac fun foam ■ pink floral printed paper ■ pink card ■ white linen-effect card ■ white linen-effect folded card 12.5cm (5in) square ■ large square punch ■ white gel pen ■ 4 pale pink brads

Stamp a small stamp, such as a flower, into hot fun foam, to recess the image, cut out and use as a stamp to print a reversed version of the original.

1 Using scissors, trim the fun foam slightly larger than the wood mount of the stamp. Heat the surface with a heat gun until it begins to bow very slightly. Press the stamp firmly down into the surface. Hold for a few seconds, then lift the stamp off. Check that you have made an even print.

2 Using a sponge dauber, apply purple ink lightly across the surface of the foam. As the ink goes over the areas in relief, the outline of the elephant, which is in recess, will begin to show more. Cut out the elephant, leaving a very narrow border around the recessed outline.

3 Punch five squares from the printed paper and four from pink card. Draw a stitched line around the edges of the pink squares with the white pen. Arrange to form one large square. Cut a piece of white card slightly larger. Mount the squares on the white card.

4 Cover the folded card with the printed paper. Punch a hole in each corner of the patchwork square with a 1.5mm (1/16in) holepunch. Insert the brads. Mount on the folded card with adhesive foam pads. Stick the elephant to the patchwork square with Hi-Tack Glue™.

Stitching

Stitching can be used on card to great effect. Hand stitching is ideal for enhancing a stamped design by adding extra details, as well as creating interesting frames and outlines. As card doesn't stretch like fabric, you need to take into account the size and spacing of the holes in relation to the size of the needle and thickness of the thread. For instance, if the holes are too close together, the card could split when stitching.

You will need ■ pair of hearts rubber stamp ■ graphite black Brilliance™ inkpad ■ black fine line pen ■ silver pen ■ Sakura Gelly Roll Glaze™ pens – pink, black ■ white and black card ■ thin, semi-transparent white paper ■ silver linen-effect card ■ black, silver and grey printed paper ■ white linen-effect folded card 16 x 11cm (6¼ x 4½in) ■ silver thread and sewing needle ■ corner heart punch

1 Using the inkpad, stamp the image onto white card. Re-ink and stamp onto the white paper. Draw in the strings and evenly spaced dots with the fine line pen – try out the spacing on scrap card with the needle and thread to see if it is workable.

2 Place the paper over the card and align the hearts. Working on a foam mat, use a paper piercer to make small holes through both the scrap paper and card. Do not attempt to widen the holes at this stage, as you need to be able see the card to do this.

3 Remove the paper and use the paper piercer to enlarge the holes. Refer to your test piece for the correct size and check it carefully – if you have to tug hard on the needle, you may crease the card.

Transform a simple stamped motif into a unique image by adding hand-stitched detail.

Here, a pair of hearts have been given dangling strings, hand stitched in silver thread and tied together with a thread bow, to create a fun yet romantic design. I chose bright, funky colours to complement the contemporary style of the hearts. Do be sure to plan beforehand on scrap paper where to put the stitching, rather than working freehand.

For a fun variation, the stamped hearts could be hanging from hand-stitched strings coming down from the top of the panel.

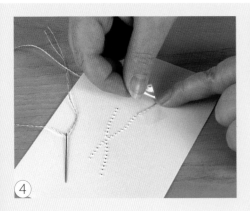

④

⑤

⑥

4 Secure the silver thread to the card back with a small piece of adhesive tape before you start stitching – a knot may get in the way when you layer up the panel. Do not pull too hard when you begin stitching, otherwise you could release the thread.

5 Use the sewing needle to sew backstitches through the holes – avoid pulling too hard, otherwise the card could split between the stitches. When you have completed the stitching, secure the other end of the thread with a small piece of adhesive tape to the card back.

6 Colour in the silver areas on the hearts first, as the silver pen dries more quickly. Colour in the pink areas with the glaze pen and allow to dry before using the black glaze pen. The pink and black areas will remain glossy when dry.

(7)

7 Trim the white card to 11.5 x 7.5cm (4½ x 3in). Tie a length of silver thread in a bow. Apply a tiny dot of Hi-Tack Glue™ to the back of the knot and stick over the point where the balloon strings cross over.

(8)

8 Using the corner punch, punch out a selection of tiny hearts from silver and black card. Use a pencil dot to mark where you want the hearts to go on the panel. Apply a tiny dot of Hi-Tack Glue™ over each mark and stick the hearts in place.

(9)

9 Mount the panel on a slightly larger piece of black card. Glue a wide strip of the printed paper down the left-hand side of the folded card. Glue a thin strip of black card against the edge. Cut a piece of silver card 13 x 9cm (5 x 3½in) and mount on the card. Attach the balloon panel with adhesive foam pads.

66 Give Us a Hug

Create an eye-catching background for a stamped image with stitched motifs.

Hearts punched from printed paper and outlined in backstitch, along with stitched kisses, add interest to this Father's Day design.

You will need ■ daddy and baby bear rubber stamp ■ pearlescent rust Brilliance™ inkpad ■ cream pearlescent card ■ red printed papers ■ pale blue folded card 15.5 x 10.5cm (6¼ x 4¼in) ■ medium heart punch ■ red and blue embroidery threads and sewing needle

1 Stamp the image onto the cream card. Using a wet paintbrush, pick up some of the ink from the side of the pad and paint shading on the bears and a little ground around the big bear's feet.

2 Trim the card to 15 x 10cm (6 x 4in). Punch two hearts from printed papers and glue to the panel. Pierce holes around the edges of the hearts with a paper piercer. Use the needle and the red thread to sew backstitches through the holes. Secure the thread ends with small pieces of adhesive tape to the card back.

3 Use a pencil to mark the positions of the kisses. Pierce holes with the paper piercer and rub out the marks before stitching the kisses in blue thread. Secure the thread ends as in Step 2. Mount the panel on the folded card.

You could use other punched shapes in the same way, such as stars or flowers.

67 The Witch's Cat

(23)

Extend a stamped Halloween design by adding stitched elements combined with punched shapes.

The cat and pumpkin stamped image in this design has been enhanced by hand-stitched vines and punched leaves to fill a landscape-shaped folded card.

For a variation on the design, stitch a moon and stars in place of the vines.

You will need ■ cat and pumpkin rubber stamp ■ brush markers – orange, brown, black, green ■ cream, green, orange, black and beige card ■ thin, semi-transparent white paper ■ black folded card 15 x 11cm (6 x 4½in), fold at the top ■ green embroidery thread and sewing needle ■ small leaf punch ■ die-cutting tool and witch's hat and broom dies ■ holographic glitter glue

1 Using brush marker tips, apply colour to the stamp's rubber. Breathe over the rubber and check that it is shiny before printing onto cream card. Use a wet paintbrush to dilute the colours at the pumpkin base. Spread out to create some ground. Re-ink and print onto the paper. Draw in the vines in pencil.

2 Place the paper over the card and align the pumpkins. Working on a foam mat, make holes with a paper piercer in the vines through the paper and card. Widen with the piercer. Sew backstitches in green thread. Punch leaves from green card. Stick in place, slipping some stalks under the stitching.

3 Paint orange marker diluted with water over the background. Trim to 9 x 13.5cm (3½ x 5¼in). Mount on a slightly larger piece of orange card, then onto the folded card. Die-cut and assemble a witch's hat and broom. Mount with adhesive foam pads. Highlight the cat and pumpkin with the glitter glue.

68 For Unto Us

Use a hemstitched border to create a decorative frame for a stamped design.

Although a basic stitch, hemstitch sewn in a contrasting thread makes a strong impact in this cute Nativity design. The large punched star perfectly spotlights the holy family.

Use embroidery thread for your stitching, as you can split the threads and use the thickness you want for the design.

You will need ■ chick family rubber stamp ■ graphite black Brilliance™ inkpad ■ brush markers – yellow, orange, turquoise, brown ■ white, pale yellow and yellow card ■ turquoise card 9cm (3½in) square ■ white folded card 10.5 x 13cm (4¼ x 5in) ■ pale yellow embroidery thread and needle ■ punches – jumbo star, tiny star ■ blue narrow satin ribbon

1 Using the black inkpad, stamp the chick family onto white card. Run each brush marker over a plastic lid. Dip a fine paintbrush into clean water, pick up some of the ink and use to colour in the image. Cut out the stamped image, leaving a narrow border all the way round.

2 Working on a foam mat, pierce holes around all four sides of the turquoise card 1cm (³⁄₈in) apart with a paper piercer. Widen the holes if necessary. Using pale yellow embroidery thread, sew hemstitches through the holes.

3 Punch and mount a large pale yellow star on the stitched panel. Make up a panel 9.5 x 12cm (3¾ x 4¾in) from pale yellow and yellow card. Glue to the folded card. Mount the stitched panel on the card. Attach the chick family with adhesive foam pads. Add tiny punched stars and ribbon tied around the card in a bow.

Enamelling

As well as providing a raised surface over a stamped image, embossing powder can be used as a coating over larger areas of thick card. The coating can be left intact like a glaze or you can stamp into the surface while it is still hot and in a state of flux. To make the layering process involved quick and easy, the type of embossing powder used in this technique, known as enamelling powder, is more granular in texture than that used in the heat embossing technique (see pages 28–31).

You will need ■ ringbound notebook ■ blossom rubber stamp ■ copper Encore Metallic™ inkpad ■ VersaMark™ inkpad ■ clear enamelling powder ■ embossing powders – pearlustre champagne, ruby, orange glitter ■ Stampendous Black Mini Matt™ (Retro set) ■ craft wire ■ beads ■ old baking tray and non-stick craft sheet ■ round-nosed pliers

①

②

③

1 Punch four holes down the side of the Mini Matt™ with a 4mm (⅛in) holepunch. Press down firmly on the copper inkpad until covered with ink. Pour the enamelling powder into a shallow container. While still wet, dip the mat into the powder to cover, then shake off any excess.

2 Use a piece of thick card or a wooden board to protect your work surface from the heat. Place the mat in an old baking tray lined with a non-stick craft sheet. Using a heat gun, heat the powder until it has completely melted and starts to spread. The first layer will not cover all of it.

3 While the mat surface is still hot, dip it back into the powder, holding it by its sides. Repeat Step 2, then the whole process again. If too hot to hold, leave it in the tray and use a spoon to sprinkle over the powder. Heat as in Step 2, turn the heat gun off and sprinkle with more powder.

Sprinkle embossing powders over several layers of clear enamelling to create a jewel-like effect.

For this technique, you must work on mountboard, chipboard or, as in this case, a Mini Matt™, since the intense heat will buckle ordinary card. This decorative panel has been built up from three to four layers of clear enamelling powder, coloured with embossing powders and impressed with a flower stamp. Always punch holes before you start enamelling.

You must work quickly, as any powder that does not melt will get blown away when you start heating again.

④ ⑤ ⑥

4 Three to four layers should be enough to cover the mat. When you heat the surface, you should see movement in the molten plastic but no little pit holes. Use a tiny spoon to sprinkle a little of each embossing powder at a time at random over the mat, melting after each application.

5 Using the copper inkpad, ink up the stamp. If necessary re-heat the mat until the powder is in a state of flux. Press the stamp firmly into the hot enamel surface. Hold in place for at least 20 seconds to allow the enamel to cool and solidify.

6 Add beads to a length of wire as you coil it through the holes. Curl the ends with round-nosed pliers. Using the VersaMark™ inkpad, stamp the flower at random over the notebook cover. Mount the enamelled panel with adhesive foam pads.

70 Butterfly Brooch

Make a unique item of jewellery by stamping a motif in relief into molten layers of enamelling.

Although enamel powders come in a range of colours, the clear variety is most versatile and can be easily coloured with an embossing powder, as in this striking brooch.

You will need ■ butterfly rubber stamp ■ VersaMark™ inkpad ■ green Encore Metallic™ inkpad ■ clear enamelling powder ■ Aqua Tinsel™ embossing powder ■ Stampendous black Mini Matt™ (Circles and Ovals set) ■ black card 16 x 8cm (6¼ x 3¼in) ■ blue printed paper ■ craft wire ■ beads ■ blue fibres ■ brooch pin ■ old baking tray and non-stick craft sheet ■ round-nosed pliers

If the enamelling runs off the sides of the mat, use small, sharp scissors to trim it back.

1 Punch three holes down the side of the Mini Matt™ with a 4mm (⅛in) holepunch. Press down on the VersaMark™ inkpad until covered with ink. While still wet, dip into the enamelling powder to cover. Shake off any excess.

2 Using a heat gun, heat the powder until completely melted and starting to spread. While still hot, dip back into the powder. Melt the second layer, then repeat the process to apply a third layer.

3 If necessary re-heat the enamelling, sprinkle with a little embossing powder and melt. Stamp the butterfly into the enamel with green ink.

4 Add beads to the wire as you coil it through the holes. Curl the ends. Trim the black card to make a tag. Add pieces of printed paper. Punch a hole with a 6mm (¼in) holepunch. Thread with fibres. Stick a brooch pin to the butterfly with Hi-Tack Glue™. Mount with adhesive foam pads.

71 Sunshine Pin

Use several layers of melted enamel powder to add a glaze to a stamped card tile.

I used mountboard for this brooch so that a section of a larger stamped image could be cut out, rather than trying to find an image to fit.

You will need ■ garden sampler rubber stamp ■ graphite black Brilliance™inkpad ■ VersaMark™ inkpad ■ clear enamelling powder ■ colouring pencils ■ pink brush marker ■ white mountboard ■ holographic glitter ■ craft wire ■ beads ■ brooch pin ■ non-stick craft sheet

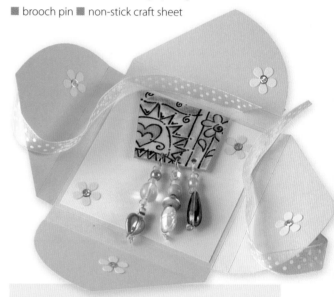

You can make or buy a box for your special gift in coordinating colours, and decorate with punched flowers with holographic dot centres, as shown.

1 Using the black inkpad, stamp the garden sampler onto mountboard. Working on a cutting mat, use a craft knife and metal ruler to cut out a section of the image. Colour in with colouring pencils. Run the brush marker along the edges and punch three holes along the bottom with a 4mm (⅛in) holepunch.

2 Press onto the surface of the VersaMark™ inkpad, then dip into the enamelling powder. Protect your work surface and place a non-stick craft sheet under the brooch. Use a heat gun to melt the enamelling powder. While the surface is still hot and in a state of flux, dip the tile back into the powder. Heat as before, then sprinkle in the glitter.

3 Two layers of enamelling should be enough to create a glaze. Thread a double length of wire through each hole. Add the beads and curl the wire ends around a cocktail stick. Stick a brooch pin to the back of the brooch with Hi-Tack Glue™.

Create a linoleum effect on a card tile using a single layer of enamelling powder.

A single stamp was used to create this dainty card, from which sections were cut and rearranged in a pleasing layout. As you need to use thick material such as mountboard for this technique, the tile effect is instant.

You will need ■ framed floral images rubber stamp ■ graphite black Brilliance™ inkpad ■ bisque VersaColor™ inkpad ■ VersaMark™ inkpad ■ clear enamelling powder ■ colouring pencils ■ white mountboard ■ beige card 10.5 x 5cm (4¼ x 2in) ■ olive green card ■ pale pink folded card 19 x 9cm (7½ x 3½in) ■ non-stick craft sheet

Use brush markers instead of pencils to achieve a bolder look, but take care, as the layer of melted powder can make the colours run.

1 Using the black inkpad, print the stamp twice onto mountboard. Colour in one whole image and just the small leaf square of the other with colouring pencils. Sponge with random patches of bisque ink. Cut out with a craft knife, leaving a narrow border. Cut the complete image in half.

2 Run a colouring pencil around the edges of each tile. Press each tile in turn onto the surface of the VersaMark™ inkpad, making sure that they are completely covered. You must use a clear ink if you want the colours to stay the same; with a tinted inkpad, any white areas will change colour.

3 Dip each tile in the enamelling powder. Shake off any excess. If it will not stick in places, use a VersaMark™ pen to touch up, then re-dip. Protect your work surface and use a non-stick craft sheet under each tile. Use a heat gun to melt the powder – it will look uneven and textured.

4 Mount the beige card on a slightly larger piece of olive green card. Stick the larger tiles on the panel with Hi-Tack Glue™ and mount on the folded card. Glue the small tile to the bottom of the folded card.

Making a Stamp

You can use a variety of materials to make a stamp – even the
humble potato! The cheapest and easiest way to make one
similar to a rubber stamp is to carve an image into an eraser.
You can also buy larger blocks of rubber for carving. If you are
not confident enough about drawing your design, you can use
a die-cutting system to cut shapes and letters from foam.

You will need ■ eraser ■ lino cutting tool and number 1 blade ■ Vivid Mini™ inkpads – spring green,
green ■ thin, semi-transparent white paper ■ white linen-effect card ■ green card ■ bottle green corrugated
card 10 x 6cm (4 x 2³⁄₈in) and 1 x 9cm (³⁄₈ x 3½in) ■ green folded card 16 x 9cm (6¼ x 3½in) ■ ribbon punch
■ yellow spotted sheer ribbon

①

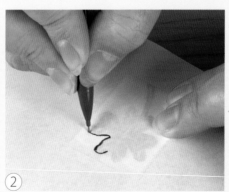

②

③

1 Place the eraser on thin white
paper. Draw around it with a
soft pencil, then draw a four-leaf
clover within the box. You need
to draw the design to produce
the print you want to achieve, so
shade in black the areas that you
want to print and leave blank
those that you need to carve out.

2 Take the completed design and
place it shaded side down on the
eraser. Rub on the back of the
paper to transfer the design onto
the eraser. Use the pencil to draw
around the outline of the leaf to
make it stand out.

3 Hold the eraser securely and,
using the lino cutting tool, carve
around the edge of the pencil
line that defines the leaf and
stalk. Don't hold the tool like a
pencil – the blade should be
flat side down so that you can
see the open 'V' shape, with the
handle tucked into your palm.

Use a lino cutting tool to carve a simple image into an ordinary stationery eraser to create a unique stamp.

In this case, it is a lucky four-leaf clover – although the motif can also be used to mark St Patrick's Day. Practise drawing the leaf on scrap paper first. Then draw a box around the eraser and transfer your design to the box, adjusting the size of the leaf as you do so. As an eraser has two sides, you can carve one side for a trial run.

> If you intend carving out letters and numbers, make sure that they are reversed on the eraser so that they print the right way round.

4 Carefully carve out the leaf detail. Once the leaf is complete, start carving out the background in a series of horizontal lines – you will find it easier to carve from the centre to the outside. Don't worry about carving it all away, as a few fine lines will add interest.

5 Print on scrap paper to see if you need to adjust your carving. Ink up the leaf with the spring green inkpad, then add random touches of the other inkpad to the edges. Stamp onto the white card. Use a fine paintbrush and water to dilute and spread the colours over the leaf and background.

6 Trim the white card to 5 x 4cm (2 x 1½in). Mount on a slightly larger piece of green card. Trim the corrugated panel to create a tag. Mount the leaf panel. Punch two slits in the tag and add the ribbon. Glue the corrugated strip to the folded card. Mount the tag with adhesive foam pads.

74 Aztec Greeting

Stamp a carved eraser over strips of coloured tissue paper for an eye-catching effect.

For an Aztec-style sun design, draw a circle with radiating points; add a spiral in the centre, and a surrounding pattern.

You will need ■ eraser ■ lino cutting tool and number 1 blade ■ graphite black Brilliance™ inkpad ■ thin, semi-transparent white paper ■ white, yellow and black card ■ yellow, pale orange, orange, pink and green tissue paper ■ pink card 8.5 x 6cm (3½ x 2⅜in) ■ orange folded card 14.5 x 9cm (5¾ x 3½in) ■ green card 10 x 4.5cm (4 x 1¾in) ■ smooth teardrop gems ■ punches – small hand, gecko

Pack an eraser, lino cutting tool, inkpad and blank postcards on your travels, carve a design inspired by your venue and create some personal postcards.

1 Draw around the eraser with a pencil onto the paper. Mark out the design in the area before transferring it to the eraser (see Steps 2–3, page 88). Use the lino tool to carve out the design. Test the print before proceeding.

2 Cover white card with strips of overlapping tissue paper – use glue stick to cover each strip thoroughly. Stamp the eraser onto the tissue paper. Trim the stamped image to the edge of the design.

3 Mount the piece of pink card on the folded card. Tear off the bottom of the green card, then mount it towards the top of the pink card panel.

4 Glue a thin yellow card strip with torn ends across both panels. Glue a row of teardrop gems along the torn edge of the green card with Hi-Tack Glue™. Attach the sun panel with adhesive foam pads, and finally, punch a hand and three geckoes from black card and glue to the card.

75 You're 18!

Use die-cut foam numbers to stamp an all-over background design.

Here, two different number fonts were used to create contrast, lightly stamped over textured card to allow the surface pattern to show through.

You will need ■ thin self-adhesive foam ■ die-cutting tool and two different number fonts, tag and star dies ■ 2 Rockers™ ■ Brilliance™ inkpads – Mediterranean blue, starlite black ■ blue textured card 10cm (4in) and 11.5cm (4½in) square ■ pale blue textured card ■ silver linen-effect folded card 13.5cm (5¼in) square ■ silver linen-effect card ■ blue ribbon

1 Die-cut the two different fonts of the number 18 from the foam (see opposite). Remove the backing from the numbers and place on the Rockers™ (see opposite) – use the lines to help you arrange the numbers and make sure that they are reversed.

2 Using the blue inkpad, stamp one foam number onto the smaller blue card square at random. Apply light pressure to allow the card texture to show through. Stamp the other number in black in between. Mount onto a slightly larger piece of pale blue card, then onto the larger blue card square and the folded card.

3 Die-cut a tag from the silver and pale blue card. Assemble the tag and thread with ribbon. Die-cut the numbers and star from silver card. Glue the solid star to the tag. Mount the tag, outline star and numbers on the card, using adhesive foam pads for the tag.

Use letters instead of numbers to stamp the background.

Stamp a design using die-cut foam stamps to make an attractive Mother's Day card.

You will only need to die-cut one wing and one body for these butterflies. As each body part is stamped separately, you can alter the position of the wings on each individual butterfly. I have also added die-cut vellum wings to create depth.

You will need ■ thin self-adhesive foam ■ Quickutz™ die-cutting tool and die KS-0413 butterflies ■ 2 Rockers™ ■ VersaColor™ inkpads – turquoise, heliotrope ■ lilac card 17.5 x 8.5cm (6¾ x 3¼in) ■ white linen-effect folded card 18 x 9cm (7 x 3½in) ■ vellum ■ white card ■ small flower punch ■ 4 pale yellow brads

You can cut your own basic shapes, such as squares and triangles, from self-adhesive foam to create an all-over design.

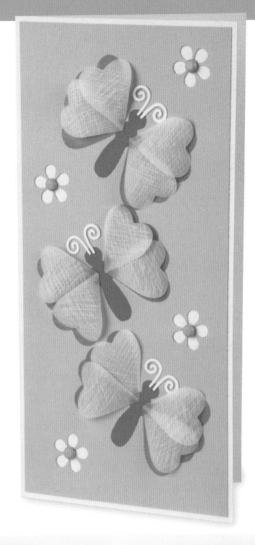

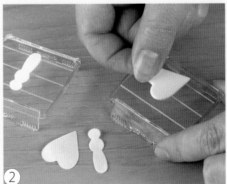

1 Make sure you remove the ejection foam from the dies before using them to cut foam pieces. Put one of the butterfly dies in the Quickutz™ tool. Slide a piece of foam in between the plates, backing side against the die. Cut the pieces from that die, then repeat with the second die.

2 Remove the backing from the butterfly body and the heart-shaped wing. Place each piece on a separate Rocker™– these are a slightly curved form of mounting block that are used with self-adhesive foam.

3 Stamp the body angled onto the lilac card with turquoise ink. With the other ink, stamp four wings, overlapping and altering their positions. Repeat twice. Punch flowers in between. Mount on the folded card. Punch holes in the flower centres with a 1.5mm (¹⁄₁₆in) holepunch. Insert brads.

4 Replace the ejection foam on the heart-shaped wing die. Cut 12 wings from vellum. Use a fine ball embossing tool on a foam mat to scribble lines across each wing – this will curl them. Apply a dot of Hi-Tack Glue™ to each wing tip. Stick to the butterflies. Die-cut white card antennae.

Style Stones & Wood

If you enjoy working on a small scale, style stones will give you plenty of scope for creativity. They come in a variety of shapes that have either a smooth surface or a recessed design. If stamping on wood has an appeal, you will need to do some initial preparation, such as sanding down and applying a thin coat of varnish or a layer of acrylic paint to seal.

You will need ■ grasses and flowers rubber stamp ■ Mica Magic™ re-fill inks – copper, jade satin ■ purple Mica Magic™inkpad ■ dragonfly style stone ■ brooch pin ■ craft wire ■ beads ■ acrylic varnish ■ wire cutters ■ round-nosed pliers

①

②

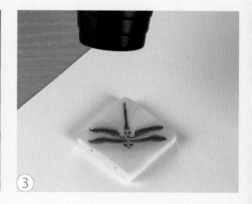

③

1 Squeeze a small drop of copper ink onto a plastic lid. Pick up some of the ink with a sponge dauber and press firmly down over the wings of the dragonfly to release the ink into the recesses. Colour the entire dragonfly in this way to achieve a smooth, even coverage of ink.

2 Dampen and fold a piece of kitchen paper into a small pad. Wipe it across the style stone to pick up the excess ink. Remove as much ink as possible, but be careful not to remove any ink in the recesses. Use the tip of a fine paintbrush to touch up the copper if this happens.

3 Heat the surface of the style stone with a heat gun to dry and set the ink in the recesses. This makes it permanent, which is important if the style stone is to be used as an item of jewellery. It also means that the ink will not lift during the next application.

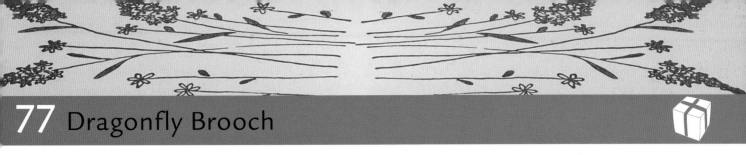

Transform a simple style stone into a special item of jewellery.

This style stone with a recessed dragonfly design was sponged with ink and stamped with part of a design to make a unique brooch. The style stone comes with ready-made holes, which can be threaded with craft wire and a selection of pretty beads to add extra decorative interest to the jewellery piece. Package the brooch in a coordinating box to turn it into a special gift.

Use a beading thread instead of craft wire and turn the dragonfly style stone into a pendant instead of a brooch.

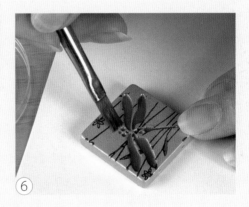

④

⑤

⑥

4 Squeeze a small drop of jade ink onto the plastic lid. Pick up some of the ink with a clean sponge dauber and gently dab over the front surface of the style stone, avoiding the recesses of the dragonfly. Heat as in Step 3. Repeat the process with the other sides, one at a time.

5 Using the purple inkpad, stamp the bottom section of the image over the front of the style stone. The stone may stick to the rubber, so carefully lift the stone off the rubber, avoiding any side-to-side movement that may smudge the print. Heat as before. Leave the style stone to cool completely.

6 Apply a thin coat of varnish to the front and two sides. Leave to dry, then varnish the back and other sides. Stick a brooch pin to the back with Hi-Tack Glue™. Use wire cutters to cut two lengths of wire. Thread through the holes, adding the beads. Use round-nosed pliers to curl the ends.

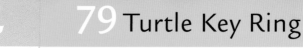

Build up layers of ink on a shaped, smooth-surfaced style stone ready for stamping.

The handbag shape of this style stone is perfect for decorating. The stamped hats and stand provide an appropriate boutique window-style context for the handbag.

You will need ■ dragonfly rubber stamp ■ hat stand and hats set of clear stamps ■ clear acrylic block ■ handbag-shaped style stone ■ Mica Magic™ re-fill inks – jade satin, purple, copper ■ lilac card 10 x 7cm (4 x 2¾in), plus extra ■ copper card ■ copper folded card 14.5 x 10.5cm (5¾ x 4¼in) ■ pale green linen-effect card 14.5 x 10.5cm (5¾ x 4¼in) ■ purple sheer ribbon

Use a folded card that is appropriate for the weight of the style stone – if too thin, the card will not remain standing.

1 Using a sponge dauber, cover the front and sides of the style stone with jade ink. Remove from the relief part with damp kitchen paper. Heat with a heat gun. Carefully apply purple ink to the cleaned parts. Heat again. Using the copper ink, print a section of the dragonfly stamp onto the stone and heat. Thread the hole with ribbon and tie in a knot.

2 Using the purple ink, stamp the stand and three hats onto the lilac card. Stamp another hat on the extra card. Using a fine paintbrush dipped into clean water, dilute the ink on the hats and colour in some of the open sections and the background around the stand. Cut out the single hat.

3 Mount the lilac panel on a slightly larger piece of copper card. Cut away a 9cm (3½in) wide section from the front of the folded card. Glue the pale green card to the back of the flap. Mount the hat panel and hat on the card, then attach the handbag with Hi-Tack Glue™. Tie ribbon around the card front in a bow.

Use acrylic paints to prepare, stamp and colour a wooden tag.

This endearing key ring would make a special gift for an animal lover. A coat of varnish after painting gives the tag a hard-wearing finish.

You will need ■ patchwork-style turtle rubber stamp ■ jet black StazOn™ inkpad ■ acrylic paints – yellow, white, purple, orange, blue, green ■ wooden tag ■ purple cord ■ key ring ■ acrylic varnish

1 Mix equal parts of yellow and white acrylic paint to produce a soft shade of yellow. Apply the colour evenly and smoothly all over the tag. As acrylic paint dries quite quickly, you may need to add water to improve the flow. Leave to dry.

2 Using the black inkpad, stamp the turtle on the tag. Mix equal parts of purple and white acrylic paint to produce a soft lilac shade and paint the turtle. Paint the shell and toes with orange and blue paint. Paint the daisy with white paint.

3 Dab green paint around the turtle to indicate grass. Add little dabs of white and orange to resemble flowers. Dilute orange paint to a thin, watery consistency and apply over areas of the sky above the turtle. Varnish the tag. Use a length of purple cord to attach a key ring to the tag.

Instead of stamping directly on the tag, stamp on paper, colour in and use the collage technique on pages 64–65.

80 Goal!

Stamp a permanent design directly onto a wooden door hanger by first sealing it with varnish.

This would make the perfect gift for a soccer-mad teenager – in fact, the design could be customized to the colours of the recipient's favourite team! The layer of acrylic varnish prevents the ink from bleeding into the wood. Make sure that you use permanent ink for stamping, so that when you apply the acrylic paints, the outline does not lift off.

You will need ■ boy soccer player rubber stamp ■ numbers and soccer accessories set of clear stamps ■ acrylic clear block ■ jet black StazOn™ inkpad ■ black permanent fine line pen ■ acrylic paints – green, white, yellow, red, pale blue ■ wooden door hanger ■ fine sandpaper ■ acrylic varnish

The final coat of varnish will make it easier to clean the door hanger.

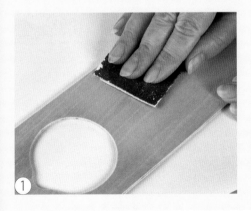

1 Check that the surface of the hanger is smooth. Use fine sandpaper to create a key in the surface of the wood so that it will absorb the varnish and to remove any small splinters that might be sticking out.

2 Using a paintbrush, apply a thin coat of varnish all over the front of the hanger. Leave to dry thoroughly. Use an acrylic varnish, as it dries more quickly and is much easier to remove from paintbrushes.

3 Using the inkpad, ink up the boy soccer player stamp and stamp the image onto the hanger. Leave the ink to dry. Use the fine line black pen to draw a grassy horizon line behind the soccer player and some tufts of grass around his feet.

4 Paint the boy, football, grass and sky with the paints. Mix a little white, red and yellow for the skin colour. Leave to dry. Using the inkpad, stamp a number on the shirt and several prints of the number above the hole. Paint the shirt number yellow. Leave to dry. Apply a coat of varnish.

STYLE STONES & WOOD 95

Fabric Stamping

Stamping on fabric enables you to create three-dimensional items that can be functional or make attractive, unique gifts. Much fun can be had adding decorative details with stitching and textile paints. If you are stamping on an item that you intend to wear and/or wash in the future, such as a T-shirt or scarf, always wash the fabric before stamping. Experiment on a small piece of your chosen fabric to test the colours and ink suitability.

You will need ■ Christmas tree rubber stamp ■ black VersaCraft™ inkpad ■ All-Purpose Inks™ – lemon yellow, tangerine, emerald, autumn leaf ■ white opal Liquid Pearls™ ■ white self-patterned cotton fabric 17 x 13cm (6¾ x 5in) ■ white card 14 x 10cm (5½ x 4in) ■ lemon yellow card 17.5 x 13.5cm (7 x 5¼in) ■ white linen-effect folded card 18 x 14cm (7 x 5½in) ■ tiny buttons in different colours ■ cream thread and sewing needle ■ yellow narrow ribbon ■ Xyron™ 510 machine ■ sandpaper

1 Iron the fabric to remove any creases. Using the black inkpad, ink the stamp up carefully. Check that there is ink all over the rubber, then stamp centrally onto the fabric. Apply a little extra pressure to make sure that there is good contact between the rubber and fabric.

2 Leave to dry. Iron to set the ink, following the ink manufacturer's instructions. Use a fine paintbrush and the coloured inks to paint the tree, trunk and star. Work from the centre out to the stamped line using small quantities of ink to avoid bleeding over the boundaries. Leave to dry.

3 If you are using wet fabric mediums to add colour, as here, you need to set the ink by ironing the fabric. Apply a small drop of Hi-Tack Glue™ inside each of the baubles. Allow the glue to become tacky to create a more instant bond before placing a button over each bauble.

Print images that cry out for embellishment onto a fabric panel and use fabric paints and buttons to bring full dimension to the decorative detailing.

For this card design, the stamped Christmas tree was coloured in using All-Purpose Inks™, then buttons added for baubles. Sticking the buttons down first with fabric glue makes them easier to stitch. As the tree is quite ornate, I chose a plain lemon mount to complete the card.

When ironing the fabric to set the ink, be sure to turn off the steam setting.

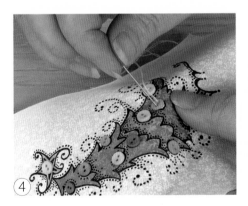
④

⑤

⑥

4 Once the glue has dried completely, use the cream thread and sewing needle to stitch the buttons to the fabric. Sewing on the buttons looks much more attractive than leaving the buttonholes blank.

5 Decide on the best position for the piece of white card in relation to the image and if necessary lightly mark the position with a pencil. Run the card through the Xyron™ machine to apply a thin, uniform layer of glue. Remove the protective backing and stick down onto the fabric.

6 Cut off all four corners of the fabric panel, leaving a 2mm (³/₃₂in) gap from each corner of the card. Apply a line of Hi-Tack Glue™ along one edge of the card and fold the fabric over tightly. Repeat for each side.

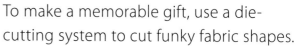

To Finish

⑦ *To mount the fabric panel onto the card, firstly distress the surface of the yellow card panel with sandpaper to reveal the white core. Then stick centrally onto the white folded card.*

⑧ *Tie a length of ribbon around the left-hand side of the front panel, finishing with a knot.*

⑨ *To create the effect of snow around and at the base of the tree, highlight some of the stamped lines and dots using the Liquid Pearls™ and leave to dry completely.*

To make a memorable gift, use a die-cutting system to cut funky fabric shapes.

Decorate with a random stamped design and sparkling beads. This is the perfect size for a pincushion and small enough to be entirely stitched by hand.

You will need ▣ leaf, stem and tendrils rubber stamp ▣ VersaCraft™ inkpads – brick, sand ▣ cream cotton fabric ▣ die-cutting tool and heart die ▣ sewing needle and burgundy red sewing thread ▣ burgundy red beads ▣ filling

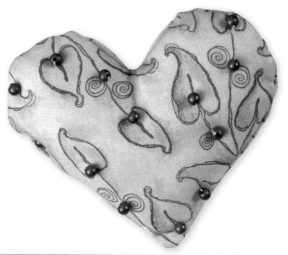

1 Cut and iron two pieces of fabric slightly larger than the heart die. Put the two pieces of fabric together, right sides facing, and use a die-cutting tool to cut a heart in both fabric pieces.

2 Place one of the fabric hearts right side up on scrap paper. Using the brick inkpad, ink the stamp up carefully. Stamp onto the fabric heart. Continue until you have evenly stamped the design. Repeat for the second heart. Using a wet paintbrush, pick up ink from both inkpads and use to highlight the leaves.

3 When the ink is dry, iron the hearts to set the ink. Sew beads onto the leaves and stems at intervals, as shown in the photo. Pin the hearts together, stamped sides facing, allowing a 1cm (⅜in) seam, then hand sew together with backstitches, leaving a 2.5cm (1in) opening in the seam. Snip from the fabric edges close to the stitching at 1cm (⅜in) intervals, then turn the pincushion cover to the right side. Push small pieces of filling through the opening in the seam, then slipstitch to close.

If you don't have a die-cutting system, you can make a card template or paper pattern to cut out shapes from fabric.

83 Daisy Needle File

Use buttons, sequins and stamps to make a mini fabric booklet ideal for storing your sewing needles – a great gift for crafters.

The all-over stamp design on the cover creates an interesting backdrop for an array of embellishments.

A die-cutting system also allows you to cut the square to the size you prefer.

You will need ■ daisy and chain clear stamp ■ clear acrylic block ■ black VersaCraft™ inkpad ■ felt fabric – 2 turquoise blue, 3 yellow squares 9.5cm (3¾in) ■ buttons – 2 butterfly, 6 round ■ sequins – 2 round, 3 leaf, 3 flower ■ sewing needle and blue sewing thread ■ embroidery thread and embroidery needle ■ pale blue narrow ribbon

1 Using the black inkpad, stamp the daisy and chain stamp repeatedly onto one turquoise blue felt square, covering the square evenly. Leave to dry, then iron to set the ink, following the ink manufacturer's instructions. Sew the butterfly buttons and sequins randomly onto the stamped square.

2 Place the three yellow felt squares between the two blue felt squares. Sew a vertical row of three round buttons close to the 'spine' of the booklet on the back and front covers to secure the squares together. Thread through each button and all the layers, then through its corresponding button. Tie in a knot on the front cover buttons.

3 Cut three short equal lengths of ribbon and fold each in half. Sew a ribbon tab to the outside edge of the yellow pages so that they are positioned one below the other when the booklet is closed.

84 Loving Iris

Experiment by stamping designs onto evenweave fabric and highlighting details with embroidery stitches and beads.

With its delicate look, this card would be suitable for sending someone wishes of sympathy.

If you are inking up a stamp using several individual pads, apply the lightest colour first, working your way through to the darkest colour.

You will need ■ iris rubber stamp ■ VersaCraft™ inkpads – cherry pink, garnet, kiwi ■ cream evenweave fabric 15.5 x 9cm (6⅛ x 3½in) ■ white card 17.5 x 11cm (7 x 4½in) ■ mottled green and purple printed papers ■ white linen-effect folded card 19.5 x 13cm (7¾ x 5in) ■ pink and green embroidery thread and embroidery needle ■ pink seed beads ■ heart charm

1 Iron the fabric. Ink up the appropriate areas of the stamp carefully with the three different inkpads. Check that there is ink all over the rubber, then stamp centrally onto the fabric. Leave to dry, then set with an iron, following the ink manufacturer's instructions.

2 Using embroidery thread, highlight details of the stamped image with a mixture of cross-stitch and running stitch, then sew seed beads to the flower stamens. Attach the heart charm to the fabric panel with a length of pink embroidery thread tied in a bow.

3 Cover the white card with mottled green paper. Cut an aperture 13.5 x 7cm (5¼ x 2¾in) in the card. Cover the white folded card with the purple paper. Mount the fabric panel behind the card frame and mount centrally onto the folded card with Hi-Tack Glue™.

Acetate & Glass

Acetate and glass both offer an exciting challenge for the keen stamper. A steady stamping hand is required, as they both have slippery surfaces. However, the results are well worth the effort. You can produce interesting overlays by attaching acetate or glass pieces to stamped backgrounds or interesting papers. Acetate can be folded into transparent cards and small glass slides can be turned into jewellery pieces.

You will need ■ graduation cap rubber stamp ■ jet black StazOn™ inkpad ■ acetate ■ pale blue textured card 12 x 8cm (4¾ x 3¼in) ■ gold linen-effect card ■ blue, white and red textured card ■ 4 gold eyelets ■ die-cutting tool and graduation cap and certificate dies ■ tassel ■ Blu Tack™

1 Using a paper trimmer or craft knife, cut a piece of acetate 16 x 24cm (6¼ x 9½in). Fold over, bring the corners together and hold firmly in place. Use your other hand to crease a fold to form the card spine, then use a bone folder to apply extra pressure along the fold.

2 Place a piece of scrap paper inside the folded acetate. Using the inkpad, stamp graduation caps at random all over the acetate. Be careful not to over-ink the rubber – as the acetate cannot absorb the ink, you are more likely to slip and smudge your print.

3 Mount the pale blue card on a slightly larger piece of gold card. Place a small piece of Blu Tack™ on the back in the centre. Position the panel on the inside of the folded acetate and use the Blu Tack™ to hold in place.

Stamp a design on acetate to create an unusual transparent folded card.

Eyelets have been used here to secure a card panel to the acetate so that no adhesive shows through the back of the card. The composition allows enough space on the inside card panel to include a personalized greeting. Although the tassel suggests a graduation theme, the design would be suitable to celebrate any academic achievement.

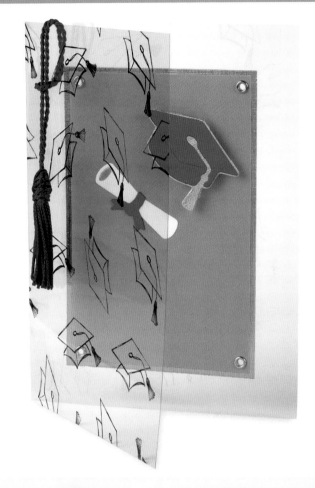

If don't like your stamping, you can wipe the acetate clean with StazOn™ stamp cleaner, but only immediately after stamping the design.

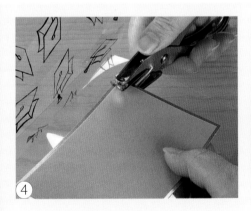

(4)

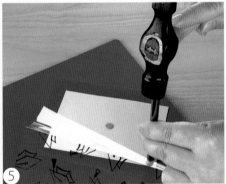

(5)

(6)

4 Punch a hole in each corner of the panel through the blue card with a 4mm (⅛in) holepunch. Hold the panel firmly in position with your hand as you punch – as the Blu Tack™ only temporarily holds the panel in place, some movement may occur.

5 Slip an eyelet into a hole, through card and acetate. Turn over. On a hard mat, place the setter over the eyelet hole. Hammer the setter a few times until the eyelet splits and flattens. You may need to flatten the eyelet back further, with just the hammer head. Repeat to set the other eyelets.

6 Die-cut and assemble the cap, using blue and gold card, and certificate, using gold, white and red card. Mount on the card panel, using an adhesive foam pad for the hat. Punch a hole with the 4mm (⅛in) holepunch through the acetate front and thread the tassel into place.

86 Cocktail Anyone?

Use permanent ink to stamp a design onto acetate, and colour in with permanent markers on the reverse.

These rows of celebratory cocktails stamped on acetate are backed by spotted paper for added interest. Glitter glue adds a touch of fizz to the cocktails.

Your cutting mat may have a printed grid that you can use as a guide to stamping on the acetate.

You will need ■ three cocktails rubber stamp ■ jet black StazOn™ inkpad
■ permanent markers – yellow, orange, magenta ■ acetate ■ spotted printed paper
17 x 9cm (6¾ x 3½in) ■ magenta card 17 x 9.5cm (6¾ x 3¾in) ■ black folded card
17 x 10.5cm (6¾ x 4¼in) ■ 5 gold eyelets ■ holographic glitter

1 Draw three horizontal lines on scrap paper 5cm (2in) apart and place a piece of acetate over the paper. Use the lines as a guide to stamp three evenly spaced rows of cocktails on the acetate with the black inkpad. Leave the ink to dry. Trim the acetate to 17 x 8cm (6¾ x 3¼in).

2 Turn the acetate over and use the markers to colour in the drinks and fruit slices on the glasses – working on the back of the acetate avoids colouring over the stamped outline and re-activating the ink. For a contemporary effect, leave some open spaces and use blocks of colour.

3 Mount the spotted paper onto the magenta card. Mount the panel onto the folded card. Secure the acetate panel to the card with the eyelets spaced out between the rows of glasses (see page 101). Add PVA (white) glue to the liquid in the glasses and sprinkle with the glitter.

87 Vintage Brooch

Sandwich a stamped image between glass slides and create a stylish brooch.

I used one slide as a viewfinder to select a small section from this 1920s-style stamp. The postmark from the design was ideal for stamping over the front slide.

Use thin layers of pen ink to allow the craft paper to show through for a vintage look.

You will need ■ 1920s-style postcard with lady and postmark rubber stamp ■ StazOn™ inkpads – jet black, teal blue ■ brush markers – grey, pink, teal ■ 2 Ranger™ glass slides 4cm (1½in) square ■ craft card ■ pale teal, teal and dark teal card ■ craft folded card 12cm (4¾in) square ■ gold tape ■ 3 gold eyelets ■ craft wire ■ beads ■ brooch pin

1 Using the black inkpad, stamp the lady on craft card. Run each brush marker over a plastic lid. Use to colour in the image with a wet paintbrush. Use a slide to select a section of the image. Draw around it and cut out. Using the blue inkpad, stamp the postmark several times on a slide. Sandwich the panel between the slides.

2 Unwind a length of gold tape. Holding the slide sandwich between your fingers, place the bottom edge on the tape. Roll the slide sandwich along the length of tape so that each side sticks to the tape. Trim the excess and, as it is wider than the sandwich, fold it over onto the glass. Use a bone folder to burnish until completely flat.

3 Make a 9cm (3½in) square panel from strips of teal card, from light to dark tones. Mount on the folded card. Set the eyelets (see page 101). Wrap wire around the slides, adding beads as you go. Secure the wire ends with a bead and curl with a cocktail stick. Stick a brooch pin to the back with Hi-Tack Glue™. Mount on the card with adhesive foam pads.

Floral Sun Catcher

Stamp a design onto a glass shape. For this technique, it is easier to take the glass to the rubber, working with the stamp upside down.

Here, a pre-cut glass diamond has been used, but there are lots of other glass shapes to choose from, such as ovals and circles. Instead of using the glaze pens to colour in the design, you could use any of the glass paints available.

You will need ■ two flowers rubber stamp ■ pre-cut glass diamond shape ■ jet black StazOn™ inkpad ■ Sakura Gelly Roll Glaze™ pens – blue, yellow, orange ■ blue fibres

Use methylated spirits to clean any greasy marks that may be on the surface of the glass before stamping.

① ②

1 Using the black inkpad, ink up the stamp. Hold the piece of glass above the rubber and use it as a viewfinder to select an area of the design. Lower the glass very slowly until it lies on top of the rubber. Press down evenly to make a print on the glass, then carefully lift the glass off.

2 Allow the ink to dry or heat very gently with a heat gun to speed up the process. Use the blue pen to colour in the flower, then use the yellow and orange pens for the background – apply the yellow first, and while still wet, add touches of orange. The edges of the colours will blend naturally.

3 Let the colours dry naturally. They will remain shiny and wet looking. If you need to add another layer of colour or you want to fill in any areas that appear patchy, wait for the glaze to dry completely, otherwise you risk creating a skin that will lift off.

4 Thread some matching blue fibres through the hole in the glass diamond and tie in a knot so that the glass can be hung up and catch the light.

Shrink Plastic

While pre-printed shrink plastic is available, you can easily use stamps to print your own designs. When the plastic is heated to shrink it, the size of the image stamped on it will greatly reduce. You can colour the designs using a range of mediums such as chalks, pencils and gel pens, but be aware that colours intensify when shrunk. Use shrink plastic to create unique jewellery, badges and key rings.

You will need ■ rubber stamps – row of flowers; dragonfly ■ Brilliance™ inkpads – pearlescent yellow, graphite black, pearlescent purple ■ Sakura Stardust™ pens – yellow, orange, purple, green, light blue ■ sheet of white shrink plastic ■ lilac textured card 11 x 8.5cm (4½ x 3½in) ■ craft wire ■ beads ■ brooch pin ■ yellow spotted sheer ribbon ■ sanding block ■ talcum powder ■ round-nosed pliers

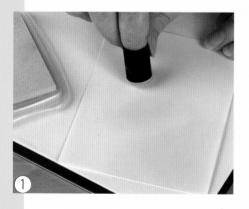

1 Cut the white shrink plastic into quarters. If it isn't pre-sanded, use a sanding block to give the surface a little texture. Using a sponge dauber, apply soft, uneven tones of yellow ink all over. Apply lightly, as colours intensify when shrunk. Remove any excess with a damp cloth.

2 Using the black inkpad, stamp the row of flowers twice along the bottom half of the plastic, re-inking the stamp between prints. Stamp the dragonfly to hover above the flower heads with black ink. Let the ink dry naturally or carefully use a heat gun at a distance to speed up the process.

3 Using the template on page 117, make your own template from frosted or clear shrink plastic. Place it on the stamped plastic and carefully move it around until you have selected your preferred section of the design. Lightly draw around the template with a pencil.

Summer Garden Pin

Create a stunning jewellery item
by stamping onto shrink plastic
before heating and threading
with wire and beads.

As the plastic tends to distort during the
shrinkage, I chose a random shape for this
garden-inspired brooch. It would make
a delightful gift for Mother's Day. To lose
the whiteness of the shrink plastic, I have
sponged it with delicate tones of yellow to
create a sunny background for the colourful
flowers and hovering dragonfly.

*If the plastic keeps being blown away as you
heat it, pin it down gently with the end of a
kebab stick or use a shallow box to contain it.*

④

⑤

⑥

4 Cut out the shape with small,
sharp scissors, cutting just inside
the outline to lose the pencil line.
Using the sponge dauber, add
stronger touches of yellow ink
between the flower heads and
the dragonfly.

5 Make three holes in the top left-
hand corner above the flowers
and four along the base between
the stems with a 4mm (⅛in)
holepunch – the plastic is too
thick to punch once it has shrunk.
The holes will shrink in size, so
they need to be large enough at
this stage to allow for shrinkage.

6 Colour in the flowers and
dragonfly with the pens
– the effect will look more
contemporary if you leave
some spaces uncoloured. As
the colours are opaque, try not
to go over the stamped outline.
Add small green dots in between
the flowers and dragonfly.

(7)

7 Lightly dust the back of the plastic with talcum powder. This will help stop the plastic sticking to itself as it curls up in the heating process. Point a heat gun towards the surface and move it around to spread the heat as evenly as possible over the plastic.

(8)

8 The plastic will curl up dramatically as it shrinks, but continue to heat until it flattens. Alternatively, place on a baking tray lined with foil and heat in an ordinary (not fan) oven following the manufacturer's instructions. This is easier for larger pieces. Coil wire through the holes, adding beads. Curl the ends with round-nosed pliers.

(9)

9 Stick a brooch pin to the back with Hi-Tack Glue™. Trim the lilac card to make a tag. Stamp with purple flowers and dragonflies. Punch a hole with a 6mm (¼in) holepunch. Thread with and tie ribbon around the tag. Mount the brooch with adhesive foam pads.

90 Dangling Dragonflies

Die-cut simple shapes from shrink plastic and decorate with sponged ink and stamping before shrinking.

The hearts for these earrings were decorated front and back, since both sides will be visible when worn. They are presented on a large die-cut heart stamped with the same design.

You will need ■ dragonflies rubber stamp ■ Brilliance™ inkpads – peacock, Mediterranean blue ■ clear shrink plastic ■ pale green textured card ■ die-cutting tool and small heart and large heart dies ■ gold wire ■ beads ■ 2 gold jump rings ■ pair of gold hook earring findings ■ holographic glitter glue ■ blue sheer ribbon ■ sanding block ■ talcum powder ■ round-nosed pliers

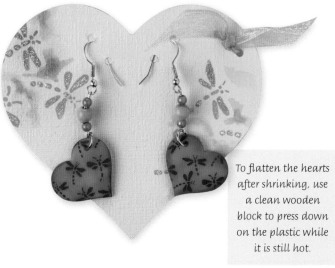

To flatten the hearts after shrinking, use a clean wooden block to press down on the plastic while it is still hot.

1 Die-cut two small hearts from the shrink plastic (see pages 40–43). Sand both sides. Punch a hole in each with a 6mm (¼in) holepunch. Sponge the fronts and backs with all three inks from the peacock inkpad. Using the blue inkpad, stamp dragonflies over the fronts and backs. Shrink both hearts individually if using a heat gun, or together in an oven.

2 Thread two lengths of wire with beads. Use round-nosed pliers to make loops in each end. Open the jump rings with the pliers and attach one to each heart. Slide a wire loop onto each ring and close up. Open up the small rings on the findings and attach the remaining wire loops.

3 Die-cut a large green card heart. Punch four holes with a 4mm (⅛in) holepunch. Use the Peacock inkpad to stamp with dragonflies. Use a fine wet paintbrush to apply the ink between the dragonflies. Thread the earring hooks through the central holes. Thread ribbon through the other holes and knot.

91 Flower Ring

Use alcohol inks to colour shrink plastic shapes after heating.

These flowers heads were strung onto wire with beads and hung around a glass vase so that the light shines through the ink colours, creating a stained-glass effect.

You will need ■ small glass vase ■ four flower heads set of rubber stamps ■ jet black StazOn™ inkpad ■ alcohol inks – yellow, magenta ■ clear shrink plastic ■ craft wire ■ beads ■ sanding block ■ talcum powder

You can use blending solution to remove alcohol ink if the colour is too intense, but only if the ink is applied to the unstamped side.

1 Sand the shrink plastic. Using the inkpad, stamp at least eight flowers – try to use each flower head twice. Cut out roughly, leaving a narrow border around each flower.

2 Make a hole in each flower with a 4mm (⅛in) holepunch. Now shrink the flowers with a heat gun or in an oven. Place the flowers stamped side down on scrap paper. Use the dropper of the ink bottle to drop tiny quantities of alcohol ink over the flowers and leave to dry.

3 Thread beads and six flower heads onto wire long enough to wrap twice around the vase, passing the wire back through each hole to secure. Wind around the vase, bring the ends to the front and thread through a bead to secure. Thread and secure more beads and the last two flowers, then twist the wire ends.

92 Cute as a Button

Make a decorative button by cutting out a stamped motif from shrink plastic, punching buttonholes and shrinking.

This cute teddy button could be created in any colour to suit the new arrival in question.

Since these buttons are strong enough to use as real buttons, make a few extra to use on a child's garment.

You will need ■ teddy bear rubber stamp ■ coral Brilliance™ inkpad ■ white shrink plastic ■ pink checked and spotted printed papers ■ white linen-effect card ■ white linen-effect folded card 12cm (4¾in) square ■ jumbo scalloped square punch ■ 2 pink brads ■ white embroidery thread ■ sanding block ■ talcum powder

1 Use the sanding block to sand the white shrink plastic ready for stamping. Using the coral inkpad, stamp the bear onto the plastic. Dab a cotton bud a couple of times onto scrap paper to flatten the end slightly, then dab onto the coral inkpad and use to stamp spots all over the bear. Leave the ink to dry. Cut out the bear, leaving a narrow border all the way round.

2 Punch two holes in the bear's tummy with a 4mm (⅛in) holepunch – do not be tempted to use a larger holepunch, as the holes will be too big for buttonholes. Shrink the bear with a heat gun or in an oven. Cut a 4.8cm (1⅞in) square of pink checked paper. Using the punch, punch a scalloped square from white card. Mount the checked paper panel on the scalloped square.

3 Cover the folded card front with an 11.5cm (4½in) square of pink spotted paper. Stick a checked paper strip across the card, punch a hole towards each end and insert a brad into each. Mount the scalloped panel over the strip with adhesive foam pads. Pass the white thread through the buttonholes and tie in a knot. Mount on the card with an adhesive foam pad.

Glossy Paper

Certain inkpads that contain dye-based inks work considerably better on glossy paper. The colours appear much brighter and almost glisten on the shiny surface. By stamping on glossy paper with clear ink, you can create a batik-like resist. Alcohol inks can be manipulated to create beautiful patterns and effects on glossy paper, making excellent backgrounds for stamped designs.

You will need ■ elephant rubber stamp ■ Spectrum Kaleidacolor™ inkpad ■ graphite black Brilliance™ inkpad ■ purple Sakura Gelly Roll Glaze™ pen ■ bubble wrap ■ Ranger™ glossy paper ■ magenta card 13cm (5in) square ■ orange and purple textured card ■ gold linen-effect card ■ white linen-effect folded card 14cm (5½in) square ■ small and tiny flower punches ■ holographic dots ■ brayer

(1)

(2)

(3)

1 Remove the lid from the Spectrum inkpad and push the individual pads together with the slide button. Keeping the pads apart when stored prevents the inks from bleeding and mixing. To prompt you to slide them apart after using, the lid won't sit properly over the base.

2 Anchor the pad down with your spare hand and ink up the brayer by rolling it back and forth over the surface of the pad. Keep spinning the roller around when it is off the pad to get an even coverage. Roll it from side to side very slightly to lose the defined colour bands.

3 Cover your work surface with scrap paper. Cut bubble wrap slightly larger than the glossy paper. Lay bubble side up on the scrap paper. Roll the brayer across the wrap gently, to avoid popping the bubbles. Go over the same section a few times to disperse and blend the ink.

93 Spotty Elephants

Experiment with taking prints from bubble wrap to make an unusual background.

For this technique, you will need to use a brayer to pick up the ink from the inkpad and for applying it to the surface of the piece of bubble wrap. You can use the interesting prints that result as complete backgrounds or you can stamp a simple motif over a small section of the printed pattern and cut out, as I have done to create this little troop of elephants.

If using a large multicoloured dye-based inkpad without individual sections, store it level to avoid the colours running into each other.

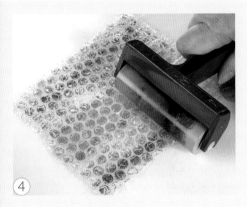

(4)

(5)

(6)

4 Re-load the brayer with ink. Turn the bubble wrap clockwise 180 degrees so that the same two colours will go over each other when you brayer the next section, otherwise you will mix a green band with the edge of an orange one, resulting in a muddy colour in the centre of your print.

5 Place the glossy paper shiny side down on the bubble wrap. Gently rub on the back of the paper with your fingers. Slowly glide over each section until you have pressed over the entire piece. Do not lift your fingers up and down on the paper, as you risk smudging the print.

6 Let the ink dry. Using the black inkpad, stamp four elephants on the background – dye-based inks dry very quickly on the glossy paper. Cut out the motifs with small, sharp scissors – you don't need to cut out the flowers, as these will be replaced by punched flowers.

To Finish

⑦ *Mount the magenta panel on a slightly larger piece of gold card and onto the folded card.*

⑪ *Add holographic dots to the corners of the magenta panel and the ends of the purple strips.*

Create a sunset effect on glossy paper using a multicoloured dye-based inkpad.

Here, the setting sun for the holiday 'photo' was created by stamping a solid circle with clear ink to act as a resist to the coloured ink applied over the top.

You will need ■ rubber stamps – large solid circle; tropical landscape ■ VersaMark™ inkpad ■ desert heat Kaleidacolor™ inkpad ■ graphite black Brilliance™ inkpad ■ Ranger™ glossy paper ■ black card ■ peach card 14 x 9.5cm (5½ x 3¾in) ■ black folded card 10 x 14.5cm (4 x 5¾in) ■ white, lime green and yellow card ■ die-cutting tool and large and small Hawaiian flowers and sail boat dies ■ brayer ■ deckle-edged scissors

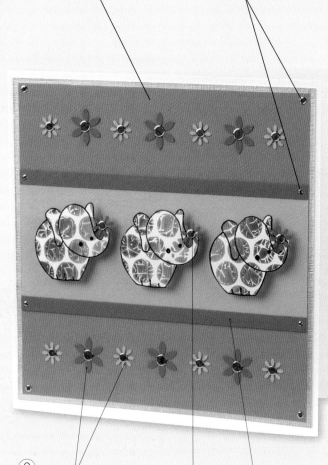

Be careful not to get any water on the glossy card, as die-based inks are not waterproof.

⑨ *Punch eight tiny orange flowers and six small purple flowers. Colour several holographic dots varying in size with the glaze pen. Allow to dry, then use as flower centres. Glue the flowers to the card in two identical rows.*

⑧ *Glue a 5cm (2in) wide band of orange card across the centre of the magenta card. Glue a narrow purple strip either side.*

⑩ *Punch a tiny purple flower for each elephant, add a coloured holographic dot and stick in place. Mount the elephants with adhesive foam pads.*

1 Cut a long strip of glossy paper almost as wide as the brayer's roller. Using the VersaMark™ inkpad, stamp a circle in the centre. Ink up the brayer with the Kaleidacolor™ inkpad. Roll over the paper several times. Leave to dry.

2 Using the black inkpad, stamp the landscape across the sunset. Trim the paper to 4.5 x 7cm (1¾ x 2¾in). Mount on a slightly larger piece of black card. Trim the edges with deckle-edged scissors.

3 Using the Kaleidacolor™ inkpad, stamp the landscape across the bottom of the peach card. Use a wet fine paintbrush to dilute the ink to create clouds and water.

4 Stick the panel on the folded card. Die-cut and assemble a large Hawaiian flower. Die-cut a leaf and a few small flowers. Mount the sunset on the folded card with adhesive foam pads. Glue the flowers and leaf around the photo. Die-cut a sail boat and mount with adhesive foam pads..

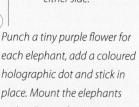

95 Tag Trio

Print alcohol inks onto glossy card with a felt pad and use blending solution to spread the colours.

If you keep adding the blending solution to the felt and use a fresh sheet of glossy paper, you can create a softer background.

Here, the resulting experimental effects were used as a background for some stamped tags, presented on larger card tags. The inks will lighten as they dry.

You will need ▓ three floral tags rubber stamp ▓ stamping block and felt pads ▓ alcohol inks – jade, plum, ochre ▓ alcohol blending solution ▓ graphite black Brilliance™ inkpad ▓ Sakura Stardust™ pens – pink, jade, purple ▓ Ranger™ glossy paper ▓ three 8 x 6cm (3¼ x 2⅜in) panels of teal textured card ▓ large and small strips of dark teal textured card ▓ craft wire ▓ round-nosed pliers ▓ stapler and staples

1 Hold the handle below the stamping block as you place a felt pad on the grip. Apply drops of ink all over the felt. Use all three colours in turn to cover. Trim the glossy paper slightly larger than the stamp. Use the block to press the felt down on the paper. Some areas may be patchy, but this is part of the effect.

2 Apply drops of the blending solution to the felt pad to re-activate the colours. Press the felt onto the paper again. The inks dilute and diffuse, creating patterns. Leave to dry. Using the black inkpad, stamp the tags on the paper. Cut out. Use the pens to highlight the flowers.

3 Trim the teal panels to make large tags. Glue a paper strip to each. Punch holes with a 1.5mm (¹⁄₁₆in) holepunch. Use round-nosed pliers to make four jump rings. Use to link the tags together. Add the folded dark teal strips to the tags, stapling the larger ones. Mount the little tags with adhesive foam pads.

96 All Dressed Up

Try using alcohol inks to produce a floral effect on glossy paper, perfect for a girl-about-town.

Alcohol inks will stain your hands and take a while to wash out, so wear protective gloves when handling.

The result will depend on the colours you choose and the way in which the inks diffuse. It creates a convincing floral fabric effect for this pretty stamped dress.

You will need ▓ dress rubber stamp ▓ stamping block and felt pads ▓ alcohol inks – green, blue, plum ▓ alcohol blending solution ▓ graphite black Brilliance™ inkpad ▓ Ranger™ glossy paper ▓ pale green and plum textured card ▓ lilac textured card 14 x 11cm (5½ x 4½in) ▓ plum folded card 14.5 x 12cm (5¾ x 4¾in) ▓ tiny flower punch ▓ die-cutting tool and bag, hanger and shoes dies ▓ gems ▓ pink sheer ribbon ▓ scallop-edged scissors

1 Using a stamping block and felt pad, cover the glossy paper with the alcohol inks and diffuse with the blending solution (see Steps 1–2 above). Using the black inkpad, stamp the dress on the paper. Cut out. Trim the hem with scallop-edged scissors. Glue a strip of pale green card behind the dress around the bottom. Trim with the scallop-edged scissors to leave a border.

2 Punch seven tiny flowers from pale green card. Glue a row of the flowers above the hem of the dress, adding some gems. Die-cut a bag, hanger and shoes from plum card (see pages 40–43). Die-cut an extra bag from a scrap of the glossy paper and swap the flap for the plum one. Glue a tiny flower to the shoulder strap and one on the bag, adding some gems.

3 Mount the lilac card panel centrally on the folded card. Glue the hanger at an angle in the top left-hand corner of the card. Wrap a length of ribbon around the waist of the dress and tie in front in a pretty bow. Using adhesive foam pads, mount the dress on the panel so that the straps overlap the hanger to look like they are hanging from it. Add the bag and shoes.

Polymer Clay

Polymer clay can be used in various ways in stamping. By pressing into the clay with a stamp, you can create the design in reverse relief. Alternatively, you can print a stamp onto the clay without pressing into it. Cookie or clay cutters can be used to cut the clay into simple shapes, and it can also be pressed into small moulds and the moulded pieces used to complement stamped designs.

You will need ▨ scroll patterned background rubber stamp ▨ silver Mica Magic™ re-fill ink ▨ blue Sculpey Clay™ ▨ tree cookie cutter ▨ silver cord ▨ silver bells ▨ white silver-edged ribbon ▨ rolling pin or pasta machine ▨ kebab stick

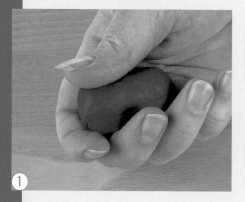

①

②

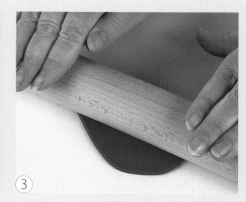

③

1 To 'condition' the clay, hold it in your hand, squeeze and knead it. Continue until it feels warm and rubbery, and has a shiny look. This is necessary to achieve the best results from the clay.

2 Whether you are using a dedicated rolling pin or pasta machine to flatten the clay, it is easier to start the process using your hands. You can encourage the clay to flatten out into an oval or round slab, depending on the final shape you require.

3 If using a rolling pin, place the clay on clean paper or a tile. Roll back and forth over the clay, pushing down gently. It will begin to spread in the direction that you roll. Keep your hands evenly spaced to avoid uneven rolling and letting the rolling pin roll off and flatten the edges.

Cut a shape from clay using a cookie cutter and impress it with a background stamp.

In this case, the shape is a traditional Christmas tree to create a hanging ornament. The silver ink is only applied to the flat surface, so that the scroll design is reversed out in blue. You can use any stamp pattern for this project, as long as it is larger than the cookie cutter. If you don't have a dedicated rolling pin or pasta machine, use a brayer or thick cardboard tube for rolling.

Be careful not to apply too much ink to the clay, as it could seep down into the recesses.

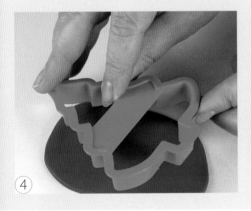

(4)

(5)

(6)

4 Place the cookie cutter over the clay at regular intervals to check your progress. You might need to change the direction of your rolling to adjust the shape of the clay. Lift the clay up at regular intervals to stop it sticking to the paper or tile. This will also help to speed up the rolling process.

5 When the clay is almost the right thickness and size, place it on the rubber of the stamp. Press down gently using your fingers to anchor the clay in place – you don't want the clay to move once you start rolling over it.

6 Use the rolling pin to press the clay down evenly into the surface of the rubber. Avoid over-stretching the clay, as you may find it difficult to lift it off from the rubber. You can work the other way round and press the stamp into the clay – see what suits you best.

7 Slowly lift and pull back the clay from the rubber. Support the back as you transfer it to the paper or tile relief side up. Avoid touching the relief side in case you flatten it or leave finger marks. You may see small stress cracks in the clay, but once it is flat again, these should disappear.

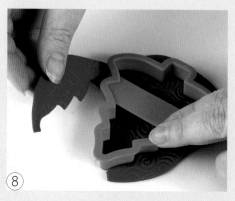

8 Use the open back of the cookie cutter as a viewfinder to select the best area to cut. Press the cutter firmly down through the clay until it touches the work surface. Check that it has cut through evenly before gently tugging away the excess from around the cutter.

9 Carefully lift the tree and hold the tip over your fingers. Use the kebab stick to make a hole, pushing it right through. Enlarge if necessary. Bake the clay following the manufacturer's instructions. Sponge with silver ink. Attach the cord, bells and ribbon.

98 Watering Can Magnet

Decorate a clay shape with a stamped design, then mount on a novelty wooden shape painted to match.

The springtime daisy design was perfect for this white clay heart and wooden watering can, fashioned into a fridge magnet for a keen gardener.

You will need ■ daisy rubber stamp ■ Brilliance™ inkpads – pearlescent lime, pearlescent orange, pearlescent yellow ■ white acrylic paint ■ white Sculpey Clay™ ■ heart cookie cutter ■ wooden watering can ■ yellow spotted sheer ribbon ■ magnets ■ rolling pin ■ sanding block

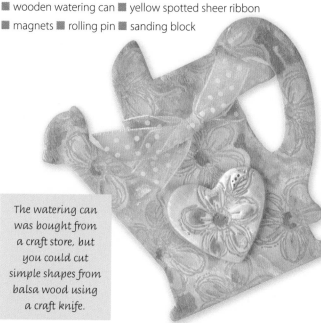

The watering can was bought from a craft store, but you could cut simple shapes from balsa wood using a craft knife.

1 Make sure that your hands are clean before conditioning the clay. Roll out the clay. Using the green inkpad, ink up the stamp and press into the clay. Don't press down too hard, to avoid the contour of the die leaving marks.

2 Use the open back of the cookie cutter to select the best area to cut. Press the cutter firmly down through the clay until it touches the work surface. Bake following the manufacturer's instructions. Leave to cool. Colour in with ink from the orange and yellow inkpads.

3 Sand the watering can to key the surface and remove any splinters. Apply a coat of white acrylic paint all over the can. Using the green inkpad, stamp daisies at random all over the can.

4 Colour in the daisies and background with ink from the orange and yellow inkpads, allowing some white to show through. Sponge the edges of the heart with green ink. Attach the heart to the can with Hi-Tack Glue™. Tie the ribbon around the can. Attach magnets to the back of the watering can.

99 Butterfly Dreams

Create a clay shape with a mould and Perfect Pearls™ for use as an embellishment.

These butterflies, moulded from pale-coloured clay as a base for the powder colours, combine well the different stamped motifs in this collage card.

To make your own pearlescent clay, make a dip in white or cream clay, add a small amount of Perfect Pearls™, close up and knead.

You will need ■ face, key and script cube rubber stamp ■ brown Brilliance™ inkpad ■ Perfect Pearls™ – rust, blue smoke, forever green ■ pale blue brush marker ■ pearlescent Sculpey Clay™ ■ butterfly mould ■ beige textured card 10 x 6cm (4 x 2³⁄₈in) ■ pale blue textured card 10.5 x 7.5cm (4¼ x 3in) ■ beige textured folded card 15 x 10cm (6 x 4in) ■ 3 copper eyelets ■ multicoloured thread

1 Condition the clay. Push into the mould until completely filled. Flatten out any clay left sticking out to a small thin flap all the way round the edge of the mould – when you pop the clay out of the mould, it will appear as if the butterfly has landed on a piece of rock. Repeat to make a second butterfly.

2 Using the dusting brush, gently apply all three Perfect Pearls™ colours to both butterflies. Try to work the powder colours into all the crevices and keep dusting until all the excess is removed. Bake the clay following the manufacturer's instructions. Leave to cool.

3 Using the inkpad, stamp the images on the beige card. Dilute with a wet fine paintbrush. Run the brush marker over a plastic lid. Apply highlights with the brush. Mount on the blue card, then on the folded card. Punch holes with a 4mm (⅛in) holepunch, set the eyelets (see page 101) and add the thread. Mount the butterflies with Hi-Tack Glue™.

100 Pearl Mask

Use a stamp to make a relief design in clay, then cut out and colour to create a 3-D ornament.

A large mask stamp was ideal for making this Mardi Gras decoration, which was sponged directly with small pearlescent inkpads.

If you don't have a clay blade, use a craft knife or any knife with a long, thin blade.

You will need ■ decorative mask rubber stamp ■ Brilliance Dewdrop™ inkpads – pearlescent jade, pearlescent orchid, pearlescent lavender ■ black Sculpey Clay™ ■ pale pink and turquoise ribbon ■ beads ■ silver cord ■ pink gems ■ rolling pin ■ clay blade ■ kebab stick

1 Condition the clay, then roll it out. Press the stamp into the surface of the clay. Don't press down too hard, to avoid the contour of the die leaving marks. Use the clay blade to cut out the mask. Make a hole in each corner with a kebab stick.

2 As the inkpads are small, you can use them as sponges to apply colour all over the mask. Allow some of the black relief detail to show through by not applying too much ink in the recesses. Bake the clay mask following the manufacturer's instructions, then leave to cool.

3 Thread ribbon through one of the holes. Put the ends of the ribbon together and thread through a bead to secure. Repeat this process with the other hole. Tie silver cord for hanging purposes to the mask, threading on some more beads. Add the pink gems to the mask with Hi-Tack Glue.™

Templates

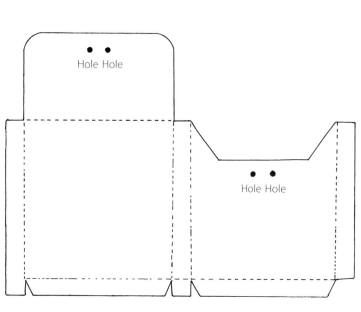

Hole Hole

Hole Hole

Flower Card Wallet, pages 32–34

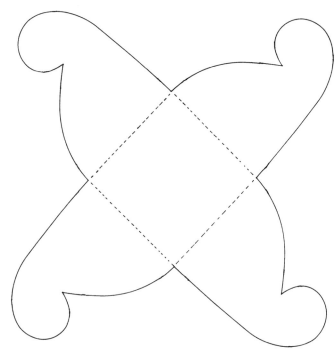

Dragonfly Box, pages 48–49

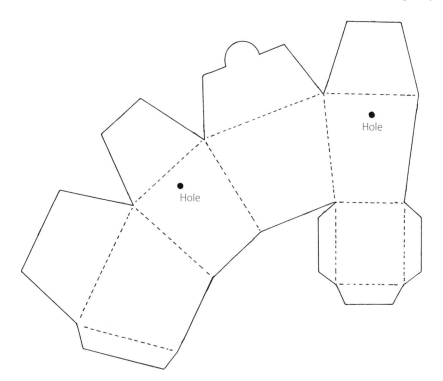

Hole

Hole

Rose Gift Box, page 58

Roaring Gift, pages 72–74

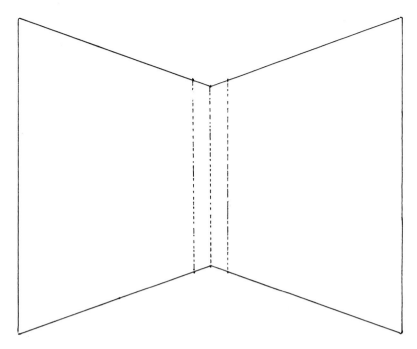

Gone Shopping, page 74

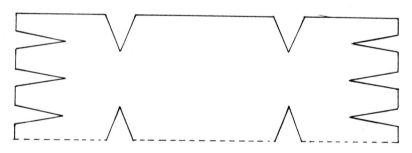

What a Cracker!, page 75

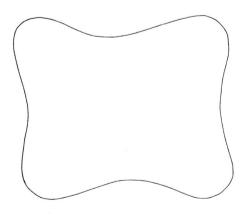

Summer Garden Pin, pages 104–106

Suppliers

The author would like to thank the following suppliers for providing copyrighted images and/or products to enable her to produce this book.

UK

F W Bramwell & Co Ltd
Old Empress Mills
Empress Street
Colne
Lancs BB8 9HU
Tel: 01282 860388
Fax: 01282 860389
www.bramwellcrafts.co.uk

Hobby Art
23 Holmethorpe Avenue
Holmethorpe Industrial Estate
Redhill
Surrey RH1 2NL
Tel: 01737 789977
www.hobbyartstamps.com

Marking World
Croftamie
Glasgow G63 0DH
Tel: 01698 812140
www.markingworld.co.uk

Woodware Craft Collection
Unit 2a, Sandylands Business
Park
Skipton
North Yorkshire BD23 2DE
Tel: 01756 700024
Fax: 01756 701097
www.woodware.co.uk

USA

Art Institute Glitter
720 N Balboa
Cottonwood, Arizona 86326
Tel: 928-639-0805
www.artglitter.com

Clearsnap Inc
PO Box 98
Anacortes, WA 98221
Tel: 360-293-6634
www.clearsnap.com

Doodlebug Design Inc
2181 California Ave Ste 100
Salt Lake City, UT 84104
Tel: 801-966-9952
Fax: 801-966-9962
www.doodlebug.ws

EK Success
261 River Road
Clifton, NJ 07014
Tel: 800-524-1349
Fax: 973-594-0540
www.eksuccess.com

Ellison
25862 Commercentre Dr
Lake Forest, CA 92630
Tel: 949-598-8822
Fax: 949-598-8840
www.ellison.com/corp

Hero Arts Rubber Stamps Inc
1343 Powell Street
Emeryville, CA 94608
Tel: 510-652-6055
Fax: 510-653-8620
www.heroarts.com

Janlynn Corp [Stamps Happen Inc]
2070 Westover Road
Chicopee, MA 01022
Tel: 413-206-0002
Fax: 413-206-0060
www.janlynn.com

JudiKins Inc
17803 S Harvard Blvd,
Gardena, CA 90248
Tel: 310-515-1115
Fax: 310-323-6619
www.judikins.com

McGill Inc
131 East Praire Street
Marengo, IL 60152
Tel: 815-568-7244
www.mcgillinc.com

My Sentiments Exactly
1045 Garden Of Gods Rd Ste L
Colorado Springs, CO 80907
Tel: 719-260-6001
Fax: 719-522-0797
www.sentiments.com

Penny Black Rubber Stamps Inc
1442 4th Street
Berkeley, CA 94710
Tel: 510-849-1883
Fax: 510-849-1887
www.pennyblackinc.com

Quickutz
1365 W 1250 S
Suite 100, Orem, UT 84058
Tel: 801-764-2000
Fax: 801-765-1199
www.quickutz.com

Ranger Industries
15 Park Road
Tinton Falls, NJ 07724
Tel: 732-389-3535
Fax: 732-389-1102
www.rangerink.com

Stampendous Inc
1240 North Red Gum
Anaheim, CA 92806
Tel: 714-688-0288
Fax: 714-688-0297
www.stampendous.com

Stewart Superior Corp
2050 Farallon Drive
San Leandro, CA 94577
Fax: 510-346-9822
www.stewartsuperior.com

Tsukineko Inc
17640 NE 65th Street
Redmond, WA 98052
Tel: 425-883-7733
Fax: 425-883-7418
www.tsukineko.com

Will'n Way
PO Box 467
97 North Main St
Coalville, UT 84017
Tel: 800-325-4890
Fax: 435-608-6331
www.willnway.com

Canada

Magenta Rubber Stamps
2275 Bombardier Street
Sainte-Julie, Quebec J3H 3B4
Tel: 450-922-5253
Fax: 450-922-0053
www.magentastyle.com

Retailers
UK

Capture The Magic
Unit 23
Northfield Road Business Park
Soham, Cambs CB7 5UF
Tel: 01353 720105
www.capturethemagic.biz

Card Inspirations
The Old Dairy, Tewin Hill Farm
Tewin, Welwyn, Herts AL6 0LL
Tel: 01438 717000
Fax: 01438 717477
www.cardinspirations.com

Craft Creations Ltd
4B Ingersoll House, Delamare Rd
Cheshunt, Herts EN8 9HD
Tel: 01992 781900
Fax: 01992 634339
www.craftcreations.com

Crafts U Love Ltd
Unit 1
West Coats Farm
Charlwood, Surrey RH6 0ES
Tel: 01293 863576
www.craftsulove.co.uk

Product Details

Craftwork Cards
Unit 2, The Moorings
Waterside Road
Stourton, Leeds
West Yorkshire LS10 1DG
Tel: 01132 765713
Fax: 01132 705986
www.craftworkcards.co.uk

Dorrie Doodle
50 Bridge Street
Aberdeen AB11 6JN
Tel/fax: 01224 212821
www.dorriedoodle.com

Sir Stampalot
Thurston House
80 Lincoln Road
Peterborough PE1 2SN
Tel: 01733 554410
Fax: 01733 554486
www.sirstampalot.co.uk

Stamp Addicts
Unit 5a, Lyon Close
Woburn Road Industrial Estate
Kempston
Bedfordshire MK42 7SB
Tel: 01234 855833
www.stampaddictsshop.co.uk

The Craft Barn
9 East Grinstead Road
Lingfield, Surrey RH7 6EP
Tel: 01342 832977
Fax: 01342 836716
www.craftbarnonline.co.uk

1 Blooming Hearts (page 16) Penny Black 2823K Pash

2 Make a Wish (page 18) Magenta 40.149. J Piece Of Cake; Quickutz Die RS-0019 Confetti

3 Blue Vases (page 19) Penny Black 3372K Vases & Flowers; Quickutz Die RS-0431 Flower

4 Funky Fish (page 19) JudiKins 2592G Cubeist Block, 6603H Funky Fish Cube; Quickutz Dies KS-0490 Retro Circles

5 Rock-a-Bye Baby (page 20) Penny Black 2073J Baby Hammock

6 Summer in Provence (page 22) Stampendous V108 Scenic Sunflower

7 Shimmering Fall (page 23) Stampendous SSC050 Glasswork Leaves Set

8 Cheers (page 23) Stamps Happen Inc 80397 White Wine Bottles; Quickutz Dies RS-0249 Wine Glass, RS-0295 Wine Bottle

9 Hats Off To You (page 24) Stampendous V107 Hattie Chick; Sizzlits Dies Hat 2 and 3

10 You're a Star (page 26) Penny Black 2307K On a Star

11 The Happy Couple (page 26) JudiKins 2379H Happy Couple

12 Thoughtful Bear (page 27) Penny Black 3458F Arrangement

13 Birthday Celebration (page 28) JudiKins 2923G Birthday Cake

14 Celebrate USA (page 30) Stampendous Y009 Stars & Stripes

15 Mighty Acorns (page 31) Stampendous F118 Acorn Square

16 Christmas Squares (page 32) Stampendous Q113 Holiday Tiles

17 Flower Card Wallet (page 32) Hero Arts LL023 Calico Blossoms, E2056 Four Small Solids, E2828 Solid Long Paintstroke

18 Home Sweet Home (page 34) Hero Arts E2797 Linear Impressions, H2922 Overlapping Geometrics, B3883 Small Dot Circle, LL892 Artistic Sketches; Sizzix Large Die Home Sweet Home 3

19 Sentiments Folder (page 35) Hero Arts LL061 Kaleidoscope Flowers, LL065 Watercolour Shapes

20 In the Pink (page 35) Hero Arts H2088 Square Background of Nine Solids, LL892 Artistic Sketches

21 Cheese and Wine Party (page 36) Woodware Craft Collection FRCL008 Cheers

22 It's Twins (page 38) Stampendous SSC070 Peek-A-Boo Baby Set; Quickutz Die RS-0176 Rattle

23 Floral Anniversary (page 39) Stampendous SSC018 Floral Garden; Sizzlits Dies Horseshoes, Girls are Weird Alphabet

24 Anna's Card (page 39) My Sentiments Exactly Y543 Posey Caps, Y545 Letter Backgrounds

25 Bon Voyage (page 40) JudiKins 6599H Hawaiian 1 Cube; Sizzix Original Dies 38-1138 Album Cover, 38-1139 Album Page Inserts;

Quickutz Dies KS-0286 Suitcase, KS-0365 Camera, KS- 0165 Shirt, RS-0026 Flip-flops

26 Hee-Haw! (page 42) Stampendous M134 Cowboy Chick, Q079 Swirling Star; Sizzix Original Dies 38-1158 Frame, Slide Holder; Sizzlits Dies Cacti, Horseshoes; Quickutz Dies RS-0170 Boot, RS-0152 Hat

27 Birthday Cake (page 43) Magenta 18.066E Heart, Star and Spiral; Sizzix Original Die 38-0997 Doodlebug Birthday Cake; Quickutz Die KS-0497 Cupcake

28 Colour Tags (page 43) Stampendous H197 Snail Fluffles, F133 Flower Fluffles; Penny Black 2354F Hedgy Flavor, 1758E Garden Buggy; Azadi Earles G970 Smiling Sun, F483 Jack in the Box; Sizzix Original Dies 38-0948 Tag, Super Crescent; Quickutz Dies RS-0287 Antique Key, KS-0407 Comb, RS-0095 Ducky, KS-0447 Truck, RS-0440 Leaves, RS-0024 Grass, KS-0055 Present, RS-0017 Balloon, RS-0100 Crayon, RS-0148 Cap, KS-0068 Frozen Treat, KS-0110 Strawberry

29 Cheeky Ghouls (page 44) Stampendous P051 Giggly Ghoul; Quickutz Dies RS-0192 Spider, RS-0082 Bats

30 Caught Out (page 46) Stampendous MTC02 Open Frames Mini Quad Cube, F133 Flower Fluffles

31 Bumblebee Blooms (page 47) Will'n Way Big Bloom Clear Stamp Set WWST-8811

32 Ahoy There! (page 47) Woodware Craft Collection FRCL037 By The Sea

33 Dragonfly Box (page 48) Magenta 23521.F Small Dragonfly

34 Poppy Field (page 50) Stampendous H203 Scenic Poppy

35 Blue Flowers (page 50) Penny Black 3365K Casual

36 Champagne Bubbles (page 51) Penny Black 2098H Bubble of Joy; Quickutz Die RS-0099 Bubbles; Ellison Thin Cuts Champagne Bottle & Cork

37 Red Rosebuds (page 52) Hero Arts LL071 Wedding Day; Quickutz Dies KS-0451, RS-0449 Heart Tag

38 Polar Fun (page 54) Hobby Art Sleigh Bear LT05 F

39 In Our Thoughts (page 55) JudiKins 2912H Lilies; Ellison Thin Cut Cross

40 Flower Jewel (page 55) Hobby Art Jewel 1393 G Diamonds

41 Christmas Peace (page 56) Penny Black 3054K Xmas Light

42 Rose Gift Box (page 58) Magenta K04420 Rose

43 Budding Artist (page 59) Penny Black 3202K Portraiture; Quickutz Die RS0103 Snail

44 Peacock Feather (page 59) Stampendous N030 Peacock Feather

45 Loving Bears (page 60) Hobby Art Paw in Paw LT08F; Sizzix Large Die Oval

Acknowledgments

A special thank you to all the team who worked very hard on my book to make it a success: Cheryl, commissioning editor; Bethany, desk editor; Emma, designer; Jo, project editor; Karl, photographer. All have been very patient and supportive.

To all the companies who supplied me with products and copyrighted images to enable me to complete and produce this book, a big thank you.

I am continually grateful for the support of my family, especially my husband Paul, whose patience is almost saintly, Liam my wonderful son, my very precious mum and dad, Malcolm and Andrew my two big brothers, John my father in law and the Read clan.

I have made a lot of good friends in the crafting world and met many people who are inspiring and very special. I feel very privileged to know them. I would like to thank all the retailers who have invited me over the years to demo or run workshops and also all the wonderful ladies and occasional gents who support these events. You make what I do worthwhile and rewarding.

Last be not least, a big thank you for the support from one very special company and the lady who runs it with her dedicated staff: Judith Brewer and Woodware.

About the Author

Françoise Read has been stamping for more than 14 years and designing stamps for over 11 years. Françoise was teaching arts and crafts at secondary school level when she first caught the rubber stamping bug. She has designed stamps for both British and American companies, and is currently in-house designer for Woodware in the UK. Françoise's love of designing has led her to use her creative ideas to develop a range of outline stickers and background papers as well as card embellishments. Françoise writes and creates for various magazines, including *Crafts Beautiful*, *Quick & Crafty* and *Card Making and Paper Crafts*. Françoise's work has been featured in several other stamping books, including two of her own: *Brilliant Birthdays* and *The Rubber Stamper's Bible*. Françoise also runs workshops for stampers and retailers, and demonstrates regularly across the UK. She has a design studio at her home in Berkshire, England, where she lives with her husband Paul and son Liam.

Index